Landmarks of world lit

C000143044

William Wordsworth

THE PRELUDE

Landmarks of world literature

General Editor: J. P. Stern

WILLIAM WORDSWORTH

The Prelude

STEPHEN GILL

*Reader in English Literature, University of Oxford
and Fellow and Tutor of Lincoln College*

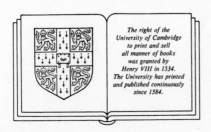

The right of the
University of Cambridge
to print and sell
all manner of books
was granted by
Henry VIII in 1534.
The University has printed
and published continuously
since 1584.

CAMBRIDGE UNIVERSITY PRESS

Cambridge
New York   Port Chester
Melbourne   Sydney

Published by the Press Syndicate of the University of Cambridge
The Pitt Building, Trumpington Street, Cambridge CB2 1RP
40 West 20th Street, New York, NY 10011-4211, USA
10 Stamford Road, Oakleigh, Melbourne 3166, Australia

First published 1991

Printed in Great Britain at the University Press, Cambridge

British Library cataloguing in publication data
Gill, Stephen 1941–
William Wordsworth: the Prelude. – (Landmarks of world
literature).
1. Poetry in English. Wordsworth, William, 1770–1850
I. Title   II. Series
821.7

Library of Congress cataloguing in publication data
Gill, Stephen Charles.
  William Wordsworth – the Prelude / Stephen Gill.
     p.   cm. – (Landmarks of world literature)
Includes bibliographical references.
ISBN 0 521 36218 0 – ISBN 0 521 36988 6 (pbk.)
1. Wordsworth, William 1770–1850. Prelude.   I. Title.
II. Series.
PR5864.G55   1991
821'.7 – dc20   90–27215   CIP

ISBN 0 521 36218 0 hardback
ISBN 0 521 36988 6 paperback

Contents

Chronology

	Wordsworth's life and publications	Important literary events	Important historical events
1770	William Wordsworth (W) born 7 April at Cockermouth		
1771	Dorothy Wordsworth (DW) born 25 September at Cockermouth		
1774		Goethe's *Werther*	
1776			American Declaration of Independence
1778	Mother, Ann Wordsworth, dies c. 8 March	Deaths of Voltaire and Rousseau. Herder's *Volkslieder*	
1779	W enters Hawkshead Grammar School, lodging with Hugh and Ann Tyson		
1780		Wielands' *Oberon*	
1781		Rousseau's *Confessions*, Schiller's *Die Räuber*	
1783	Father, John Wordsworth, dies 30 December		End of war of American Independence
1785–6	First surviving verses, *Lines written as a School Exercise at Hawkshead* (1785) and more sustained composition towards *The Vale of Esthwaite*, not published by W	Cowper's *The Task* (1785); Burns's *Poems* (1786) Goethe's *Egmont* (1788); Blake's *Songs of Innocence* (1789)	
1787	W's first published poem, *Sonnet, on Seeing Miss Helen Maria Williams Weep at a Tale of Distress* appears in *The European Magazine* in March. October: W enters St John's College, Cambridge		

1788–9	Composition of *An Evening Walk*, published 1793	Beginning of French Revolution. Storming of Bastille, 14 July 1789
1790	Walking tour in France and Switzerland with Robert Jones, July–October	*Fête de la Fédération* in France, 14 July
1791–2	W in London. In November 1791 returns to France and sees Revolutionary fervour in Paris. Is influenced by Michel Beaupuy. Love affair with Annette Vallon and birth of their daughter, Caroline, 15 December 1792. Composes *Descriptive Sketches*, published 1793. Returns to England to seek a livelihood	In 1792, Louvet denounces Robespierre, but is unsupported
1793	W feels an outcast in his own country. Writes, but does not publish, a seditious *Letter to the Bishop of Llandaff* and after wandering penniless across Salisbury Plain into Wales, composes *Salisbury Plain*. Sees Tintern Abbey	Execution of King Louis XVI, 21 January. Declaration war between Britain and France, 1 February

Godwin's *An Enquiry Concerning Political Justice* |
| 1794 | W reunited with DW in stay at Windy Brow, Keswick. In August–September stays at Rampside and sees Peele Castle. Nurses Raisley Calvert, who leaves W £900 on his death in January 1795 | Reign of Terror and fall of Robespierre, executed 28 July. Treason Trials in London, all accused acquitted. Suspension of Habeas Corpus

Blake's *Songs of Experience*, Paine's *Age of Reason*, Schiller's *Über Naive und Sentimentalische Dichtung* |

1795	Coleridge (C) lectures in Bristol on politics and religion. W a familiar figure in radical circles in London in spring and summer and regularly visits Godwin. Meets C and Robert Southey in Bristol in August. Settles with DW at Racedown in Dorset and rewrites *Salisbury Plain*		British government moves to stifle dissent with so-called 'Gagging Acts', limiting all forms of political association and expression
1797	Completes play, *The Borderers*, and moves to Alfoxden to be nearer C, with whom period of greatest intimacy begins. First version of *The Ruined Cottage* and plans for joint composition with C		
1798	The *annus mirabilis*. W completes *The Ruined Cottage* and composes the bulk of the verse published anonymously in September as *Lyrical Ballads*. Plans for *The Recluse* first mentioned. W, DW, and C go to Germany and over winter W writes autobiographical verse, the foundation of *The Prelude*		
1799	By end April W back in England. Moves into Dove Cottage, Grasmere, in December	Schiller's *Wallensteins Tod*	Napoleon made First Consul for ten years
1800	Begins *Home at Grasmere* and probably composes lines printed in 1814 as 'Prospectus' to *The Recluse*. Works on poems for second edition of *Lyrical Ballads*, published January 1801, and writes Preface	Schiller's *Maria Stuart*, Novalis's *Hymnen an die Nacht*	French defeat Austrians and retake Italy

1802	Much lyrical poetry composed. Publication in April of further edition of *Lyrical Ballads*, with revised *Preface*. Peace of Amiens enables W to visit Annette and Caroline in August. W marries Mary Hutchinson (b. 1770, d. 1859) 4 October	Scott's *Border Minstrelsy; Edinburgh Review* starts	Peace of Amiens (war renews next year). Napoleon becomes First Consul for life
1803	Fear of invasion grows. W joins local militia. Birth of first son, John. W, DW, and C tour Scotland from mid-August. W meets Sir Walter Scott 17 September. C ill and planning to leave for better climate		
1804	Much composition, especially on *The Prelude*, enlarged after March from planned five-book structure. *Ode to Duty* and completion of *Ode: Intimations of Immortality*. C sails to Malta	Sénancour's *Obermann*, Schiller's *Wilhelm Tell*	Napoleon crowned Emperor, 2 December
1805	5–6 February: John Wordsworth (b. 1772), W's brother, Captain of *Earl of Abergavenny*, drowned. W circle very deeply affected. W completes *The Prelude*	Death of Schiller; Scott's *Lay of the Last Minstrel*, Chateaubriand's *René*	Battles of Trafalgar and Austerlitz
1806–7	Visits London. Sees Sir George Beaumont's picture of Peele Castle in a storm. W spends winter in a Beaumont house at Coleorton, Leicestershire. C at last returns,		

	much changed by ill-health. W reads *The Prelude* to him. *Poems in Two Volumes* published in 1807 and ridiculed in reviews. W composes *The White Doe of Rylstone*, but does not publish it till 1815		Peninsular war begins (1808)
1808–9	W leaves Dove Cottage for larger house in Grasmere, Allan Bank. Publishes, 1809, *The Convention of Cintra*	Goethe's *Faust*, part I (1808); Coleridge's *The Friend*, August Schlegel's *Über dramatische Kunst und Literatur* (1809) Crabbe's *The Borough*	
1810	Son, William, born 12 May. Misunderstanding leads to breach with C – healed 1812. First version of *Guide to the Lakes* published as anonymous Preface to Joseph Wilkinson's *Select Views in Cumberland, Westmorland and Lancashire*		
1811–12	Deaths of children, Thomas (b. 1806) and Catherine (b. 1808). W moves from Allan Bank to Rectory, Grasmere	Austen's *Sense and Sensibility* (1811), Goethe's *Dichtung und Wahrheit* (concluded 1831); Byron's *Childe Harold*, cantos I and II (1812)	Prince of Wales becomes Regent (1811); French retreat from Moscow begins (October 1812)
1813	Becomes Distributor of Stamps for Westmorland, a post in the Revenue Service. Moves to Rydal Mount, home for the rest of his life. Completes *The Excursion*		

Year	Wordsworth's life and works	Literary events	Historical events
1814	*The Excursion* published, prefaced by an account of the plan for *The Recluse*. Further attack by reviewers. Tour of Scotland, including a visit to the Yarrow	Austen's *Mansfield Park*, Scott's *Waverley*	Allies enter Paris. Congress of Vienna
1815	*The White Doe of Rylstone* published. First *Collected Edition of Poems* published, with Preface. The argument and classification advanced here spurs C to complete his own theoretical statement, *Biographia Literaria*, published 1817	Constant's *Adolphe*, Uhland's *Gedichte*	Battle of Waterloo (18 June). Fall of Napoleon
1816	W issues a *Letter to a Friend of Robert Burns*	Austen's *Emma*, Goethe's *Italienische Reise*	Spa Fields riots in London
1817	W, moving more widely in London circles, meets Keats	Coleridge's *Sibylline Leaves*, Keats's *Poems*	Serious social unrest in Britain
1818	W campaigns hard in the Tory interest for the General Election, to the distress of many admirers, including Keats	Keats's *Endymion*, Scott's *Heart of Midlothian*, Mary Shelley's *Frankenstein*	
1819	W issues *The Waggoner* and *Peter Bell*, written in 1806 and 1798 respectively	Shelley's *The Cenci*, Crabbe's *Tales of the Hall*	'Peterloo Massacre' in Manchester, 16 August, when militia charges crowd
1820	Publishes *The River Duddon* sequence. Tours Europe and revisits places last seen in 1790. Enlarged *Collected Edition* published	Keats's *Lamia and Other Poems*, Shelley's *Prometheus Unbound*, Lamartine's *Méditations Poétiques*	Accession of George IV
1821		Byron's *Don Juan* begins, De Quincey's *Confessions of an English Opium Eater*, Goethe's *Wilhelm Meisters Wanderjahre*, Shelley's *Defence of Poetry*; death of Keats	Greek War of Independence begins

Year		Literary events	Historical events
1822	Publishes *Memorials of a Tour on the Continent, 1820* and *Ecclesiastical Sketches*	Heine's *Gedichte*; death of Shelley	
1824–6		Death of Byron (1824); Hazlitt's *Spirit of the Age* Coleridge's *Aids to Reflection* (1825);Hölderlin's *Gedichte* (1826)	
1827	Further enlarged *Collected Edition* published	Manzoni's *I Promessi Sposi*	
1828	Tours the Rhine with C and much loved daughter Dora (b. 1804)		
1829–30		Balzac begins *La Comédie Humaine* (1829); Tennyson's *Poems, Chiefly Lyrical*, Hugo's *Hernani*, Stendhal's *Le Rouge et Le Noir* (1830)	Roman Catholic Relief Bill, Catholic emancipation in Britain (1829); Accession of William IV, July Revolution in France (1830)
1831	Tours Scotland again September – October and sees Sir Walter Scott (d. 1832) for last time	Hugo's *Notre Dame de Paris*	
1832.	Further *Collected Edition*		First Reform Bill in Britain
1834	C dies 25 July		
1835	*Yarrow Revisited* published, with important Postscript	Balzac's *Le Père Goriot*, Büchner's *Dantons Tod*	
1836	Further *Collected Edition*, revised as always	Dickens's *Pickwick Papers (1836–7)*	Chartist movement begins in Britain
1837	Tours France and Italy	*Carlyle's The French Revolution*, Eichendorff's *Gedichte*	Accession of Queen Victoria
1838	Sonnets gathered into one volume		
1839	Revises *The Prelude* for the last time	Stendhal's *La Chartreuse de Parme*	National Chartist Convention in London. Riots in other parts of Britain

1842	*Poems, Chiefly of Early and Late Years* published, containing revisions of poems written in youth, notably *The Borderers* and *Salisbury Plain*. Resigns Stamp Distributorship	Tennyson's *Poems*	Further riots after Parliament again rejects Chartist Petition. Social conditions in the industrial areas worsen – the 'hungry forties'
1843	Becomes Poet Laureate on Robert Southey's death. W now a widely celebrated figure, having received honorary degrees from Durham and Oxford. Steady increase in American reputation	Ruskin begins *Modern Painters* (concluded 1860)	
1844–6	Supervises with great care preparation of one-volume *Collected Edition*, published 1845, and the final edition in six volumes, published 1849–50	Browning's *Dramatic Romances*, Mérimée's *Carmen*, Poe's *The Raven and Other Poems* (1845); Dickens's *Dombey and Son* (1846–8)	Crisis of Oxford Movement. John Henry Newman joins Roman Catholic Church (1845)
1847	W deeply stricken by the death of Dora, 9 July	Thackeray's *Vanity Fair* (1847–8)	
1848–9		Arnold's *Strayed Reveller and Other Poems*, Ruskin's *Seven Lamps of Architecture* (1849)	1848, Year of European revolutions. Republican constitution in France. The last Chartist Convention in London
1850	W dies 23 April. *The Prelude* published in July by his wife and executors	Tennyson's *In Memoriam*, Keller's *Der Grüne Heinrich*, Hawthorne's *The Scarlet Letter*	

Note on the texts

The Prelude has such a complicated textual history that the title can be used to refer not to one but to three currently available poems. Their textual history is discussed in chapter 1, but the reader ought to absorb this preliminary statement before entering the main body of this book.

The Prelude was published as a fourteen-book poem in 1850. In 1926 Ernest de Selincourt published the first scholarly edition of the poem, in which, through parallel texts, he introduced into the canon of Wordsworth's poetry the thirteen-book version of *The Prelude* of 1805. This text was updated by Helen Darbishire in 1959. Her edition remains a valuable scholarly work. In 1970 Jonathan Wordsworth, M. H. Abrams and Stephen Gill added to the canon *The Two-Part Prelude* of 1799 in their edition of *The Prelude, 1799, 1805, 1850*. This edition, usually cited as 'The Norton *Prelude*' from the name of its publisher, is widely available in America and Great Britain and is the text cited throughout this book. There is a text of the 1805 *Prelude* in the Oxford Authors series *Wordsworth*, ed. Stephen Gill, which readers of this book could also use in default of the Norton text.

Advanced study of the texts of the poem, however, must now centre on the *Cornell Wordsworth* volumes, general editor Stephen Parrish, which supersede all previous editions. The three editions are: *The Prelude, 1798–1799*, ed. Stephen Parrish; *The Thirteen-Book Prelude*, ed. Mark L. Reed; *The Fourteen-Book Prelude*, ed. W. J. B. Owen.

Chapter 1

Introduction

The Prelude as 'landmark'

A landmark is defined by the *Shorter Oxford English Dictionary*, as 'any conspicuous object in the landscape, which serves as a guide'; 'an object which is associated with some event or stage in a process; *esp.* an event which marks a period or turning-point in history'. Perhaps one might add that a landmark in literary or artistic history is a conspicuous work whose particular significance reveals itself to successive generations in differing ways.

The Prelude is certainly a landmark in literature according to these definitions. In his richly informative study, *Natural Supernaturalism*, M. H. Abrams discusses Wordsworth alongside Schiller, Goethe, Hölderlin, Novalis, Shelley and Proust, as one of those European Romantic writers whose 'characteristic concepts and patterns' are most clearly 'a displaced and reconstituted theology, or else a secularized form of devotional experience'. The sub-title of *The Prelude*, 'Growth of a Poet's Mind', also directs us to another aspect of its significance as a European Romantic poem. European Romanticism is many things, but uniting all literatures and genres is a fascination with the mysteries of the human mind. In poems and plays, novels, autobiographies, diaries and letters, writers explored the abysses and peaks of consciousness, some exulting in the power of the human imagination, others registering bewilderment and *angst*, but all united in the conviction that what characterised the artist was a greater than usual capacity for suffering or joy. The human mind becomes the site of all tragedy and comedy, of all history, the scene on which is played out the continual drama of Fall and Redemption. As Wordsworth puts it, in direct confutation of Milton,

> my theme has been
> What passed within me . . .
> This is, in truth, heroic argument
>
> (III, 173–82)

a theme which demanded the attempt to find a language to record, as no English writer had done before, the processes by which, from infancy to adulthood, the mind engages with the world. Some of the passages of the poem (notably the meditation on mother and child love in Book II, beginning 'Blessed the infant babe', 237–81) are astonishing breakthroughs into the language of psychology familiar to us today; others remain firmly in the associationist idiom of the eighteenth century – but what is common to both is the intensity with which the poet seeks to recall key moments in his own development.

The *Prelude*'s emphasis on the act and the results of recollection is what also marks out the poem as a landmark of its time. Twentieth-century psychology, educational programmes which are themselves heirs of Romanticism, and the dominance of reflective modes in literature and film, have so familiarised us to the truth of Wordsworth's paradox 'The Child is Father of the Man' that it is difficult for us to register the significance of the Romantics' insistence on the importance of memory. But when De Quincey wrote in his *Suspiria de Profundis* (1845), 'Yes, reader, countless are the mysterious handwritings of grief or joy which have inscribed themselves successively upon the palimpsest of your brain; and, like the annual leaves of aboriginal forests or the undissolving snows on the Himalaya or light falling upon light, the endless strata have covered each other in forgetfulness. But . . . they are not dead, but sleeping', he was proclaiming as a prophet the freshly revealed truth, that the key to all enquiry about the human being is that nothing that matters is really lost. Rousseau's *Confessions* and *Reveries* are the great testimonies to this truth in prose. *The Prelude* stands alone in its age in verse. Memory is both the agent by which the poet explores his past, so binding together all phases of his being, and the power which retains and highlights moments of experience

which, Wordsworth avers, haunt the adult with an inexplic-
able redemptive power. They are 'spots of time' which with
'distinct preeminence' retain a renovating virtue.

Remembering and writing down memories, however, are
not one and the same activity, no matter how often the poem
suggests they are, and one of the fascinations of *The Prelude*
is the way in which it bears witness to Wordsworth's struggle
to render up the significance of his memories by giving them
form, his attempts to find language to 'enshrine' material
which resists fixity, his evasion of memories that threaten to
overwhelm or subvert the interpretative pattern being created.
Resisting the fragmentation which Thomas McFarland has
identified in *Romanticism and the Forms of Ruin* as a common factor in all Romantic experience, the poem repeatedly
draws the reader's attention to its resistance. As in *Don Juan*
(but in a different way and for different ends) the poet
displays himself making the poem, as he talks about its
origins, the shaping of particular books or the revelation of
their main themes. But the poet also reveals his struggle with
his material less explicitly at just such moments when Wordsworth is apparently being most candid, for what one can
discern throughout the poem is experience recalcitrant to the
overall pattern, which has rejected the impress of the poet's
controlling, pattern-making stamp.

Such emphasis on the poem's subjectivity, however, and on
its appeal as a self-conscious artefact which lays bare the
travail of its creation, might suggest that *The Prelude* is a
solipsistic work, an introverted exploration of realms of the
spirit, disengaged from any specific historical moment. But it
is not so. The poem is a landmark in European literature
because it records the coming into being of an individual consciousness at exactly the moment when European society was
being tortured into extreme self-consciousness through the
convulsion of the French Revolution and the Napoleonic war
that followed. *The Prelude* is both a narrative of what it felt
like to be alive in a new bright dawn of hope and the poet's
attempt, years after the event, to distinguish as finely as possible what was lost and what gained when the dawn proved

false. The French Revolution dominated European Romanticism and reverberated throughout the nineteenth century, but no single work of art registers as well as *The Prelude* does the hopes and disappointments of an individual then, or reveals as nakedly the turmoil which the collapse of hope entailed.

A landmark in European Romantic literature certainly, but in one respect an odd one. Begun in 1799, when Napoleon was invading Switzerland, and completed in its first full version in the year of Nelson's victory at Trafalgar, *The Prelude* was not published until 1850. The greatest Romantic poem appeared in bookshops with the greatest Victorian one, Tennyson's *In Memoriam*. Whereas the quintessentially Romantic *Don Juan* appeared in Byron's lifetime and so played its part in articulating aspects of Romantic consciousness, *The Prelude* had no public life until the high-Victorian period. A poem which serves to define English Romanticism for twentieth-century scholars was hidden during the Romantic period. Explaining why leads us to an account of the poem's origins and developing life and to a definition of what poem this book refers to when it uses the title never used by the poet, *The Prelude*.

The Prelude: which text?

Poems, even short lyrics, do not come into being like a finely thrown pot, intact, inviolable, once-for-all. Their first printed form fixes words which have emerged from manuscript and proof, but it fixes them only for a while. At each reprinting the poem can and frequently does change, as the poet tries to refine punctuation, diction, rhythm. Some poets (Auden is a notable example) dismember poems wholesale; most revise more unobtrusively and scholars are rightly fascinated by their second and later thoughts, but most readers are unaware of such revision and it is the case that for much literary-critical discussion pernicketiness about textual states is unnecessary. The text of *The Prelude*, however, poses a problem which even an introductory book cannot evade, for the problem is, what poem are we talking about?

A bald statement of the issues is needed here. Their significance for our understanding of the poem is discussed in the next section.

Over 1798–9 Wordsworth wrote a blank-verse poem in two parts about his own childhood and youth. He gave it no title, but Coleridge, to whom the poem was addressed, called it his 'divine Self-biography' (notebook entry, 4 January 1804). The poem was not published, but it was entered so neatly into fair-copy manuscripts and is so clearly a shaped, self-contained work, that scholars have felt justified in publishing it. It is usually referred to as *The Two-Part Prelude*. It is important to note that Wordsworth did not publish it or ever call it by this name. In 1801 Wordsworth wrote a little more autobiography and from late 1803 worked with fervour on the materials of an extended blank-verse poem about his own life. The two parts of the existing poem were cannibalised for the emerging one, which fleetingly took forms in five and eight books before resolving into a thirteen-book poem, completed in 1805. The poem had no title, though Wordsworth frequently referred to it as the poem on 'the growth of my own mind', and still it was not published. In 1804 Wordsworth declared that it never would be 'till another work has been written and published, of sufficient importance to justify me in giving my own history to the world' (letter to Richard Sharp, 29 April 1804). This other work was *The Recluse*, discussed in the next section.

Tantalising bits of information leaked out over the years about the existence of the poem and by Wordsworth's late middle-age it was well known that he was keeping back something substantial. 'What right has he to keep such things from the present generation', grumbled John Wilson in 1843. 'Surely we ought to love our own generation more than any that follows. . . It is not fair in great authors to leave their works to be published posthumously as if their own generation was unworthy of them.' But Wordsworth was not to be jollied out of his settled intention. He repeatedly returned to the poem, subjecting it around 1829 to particularly extensive revision in which Book X was divided into two, so that by the time he had finished working over it not a line had escaped scrutiny. But publication was to be posthumous. He prepared a final manuscript in 1839 of the now fourteen-book poem for his executors to publish after his death, which, as he was 69, he believed could not be far off. In fact Wordsworth lived until 1850, but when he died his executors acted swiftly. The poem appeared in the same year, under a title which they gave it: *The Prelude, or Growth of a Poet's Mind; An Autobiographical Poem*.

All three texts − 1799, 1805, 1850 − are current. This book centres on the text of 1805. The 1799 poem cannot be dealt with in detail and as a separate work in a book of this length when almost all of it is incorporated into the 1805 poem anyway. The 1850 text subjects the 1805 poem to the later thoughts of a much older and much changed poet. It has its own integrity and many scholars, particularly in America, use it on the ground that the last revised text of an author ought to be respected. I discuss the 1805 poem, believing that it is poetically the finest version, that Wordsworth in 1805 declared the poem finished, and that this landmark of English Romantic literature needs to be read in the form it took when the greatest of the Romantic poets was at the height of his powers.

The biographical matrix

A poem which expands from two to thirteen/fourteen books; which is worked on at intervals for over forty years; which is laboriously transcribed in full into five fair-copy manuscripts (ignoring incomplete working drafts), but not published in the poet's lifetime, though it is now recognised as one of the greatest Romantic poems and Wordsworth's major and also most attractive work; which is addressed to a friend who is long dead by the time it is published; which is not given a title by the poet, but given a riddling title by his widow − the prelude to what? There is evidence enough here that *The Prelude* occupied a central but strange place in Wordsworth's life and in his *œuvre*. Exploring it takes us unavoidably to the biographical matrix of the poem, but it also leads us to the point at which a more detailed discussion of the poem and the experience of reading it can begin.

The prelude to what? Wordsworth's executors were conscious in 1850 that some explanation was called for, both for the appearance of such a substantial work as *The Prelude* immediately after the poet's death and for its title. In a prefatory note to the first edition they sketched in the poem's history and accounted for the title, essentially by quoting from Wordsworth's own preface to his lengthy philosophical poem, *The Excursion*, published in 1814. There the poet had revealed that *The Excursion* was only part of a long-meditated work called *The Recluse*, and that a completed but not published autobiographical poem (now mentioned publicly for the first time) was inextricable from the larger project. Wordsworth ties together the autobiographical poem and *The Recluse* thus:

Several years ago, when the Author retired to his native Mountains with the hope of being enabled to construct a literary Work that might live, it was a reasonable thing that he should take a review of his own Mind, and examine how far Nature and Education had qualified him for such employment. As subsidiary to this preparation, he undertook to record, in Verse, the origin and progress of his own powers . . . the result of the investigation which gave rise to it was a determination to compose a philosophical Poem, containing views of Man, Nature, and Society; and to be entitled, The Recluse. . . The preparatory Poem is biographical, and conducts the history of the Author's mind to the point where he was emboldened to hope that his faculties were sufficiently matured for entering upon the arduous labour which he had proposed to himself. . . .

Wordsworth goes on to explain publicly, as he had done privately in the 1804 letter quoted earlier, that publication of the autobiographical poem will only be justified when the philosophical one is completed.

The preface to *The Excursion* was not wholly misleading. By 1850 it was no secret that Wordsworth had failed to complete his philosophical poem and readers could now understand therefore why this autobiographical poem had remained hidden for so many years. The tidy sequence which the 1814

preface outlines, however, certainly is misleading. Wordsworth presents *The Prelude* as a self-examination undertaken
to discover what his powers were, which, coming to a cheer-
ing conclusion, led to a determination to compose 'a
philosophical Poem'. *The Prelude* thus takes its place in a
satisfactory life-history in which the poet prepares himself for
a great work, writes it, and then announces the whole project
to the world on publication of the first part of it in 1814, *The
Excursion*. The evidence reveals a much less snug relationship
between philosophical and autobiographical poem and a
more uncertain gestation for *The Prelude* than that recorded
in the confident tones of the 1814 statement.

What has to be emphasised is that in the preface just
discussed Wordsworth reverses the order of events. It was the
determination to write a philosophical poem which gave rise
to the autobiographical one, not the other way about. In the
spring of 1798, exhilarated and emboldened by months of in-
timate contact with the learned, creative, above all passionate
mind of Coleridge, Wordsworth announced to friends that he
was going to embark on a poem giving 'pictures of Nature,
Man, and Society'. 'Indeed', he added, 'I know not any thing
which will not come within the scope of my plan' (letter to
James Tobin, 6 March 1798). This was a bold statement from
a twenty-eight-year-old who had written little and published
almost nothing for the last five years, who had no settled income nor home. Nor is it surprising that nothing came of the
project in 1798–9. Evicted from their Somerset lodging,
William and Dorothy Wordsworth passed the next eighteen
months in rather miserable wandering to Germany and back
before settling down for good in the Lake District at the end
of 1799. But the vision of the philosophical poem did not
fade, though its first fruits were not 'pictures of Nature, Man,
and Society', but an intensely written, highly original
autobiographical work, *The Two-Part Prelude*, written from
late 1798 through 1799.

This marvellously rich poem is essentially a hymn of exulta-
tion, a self-projection written in the certainty that Coleridge,
to whom it is addressed, would understand its nature. On the

face of it what Wordsworth looked at when he examined his own life ought to have given little cheer. For nearly ten years he seemed to have wasted his life. Throwing away chances of advancement at Cambridge he had lived aimlessly in France, fathering a child he could not support. He had toyed with various ideas for employment, had skirted radical political circles, had written and published little and had depended upon the timely aid of friends for income and housing. In the eyes of the relatives who had supported the orphaned boy, Wordsworth seemed, to put it at its kindest, directionless. But by 1798 Wordsworth was convinced that these facts, which could not be denied, were irrelevant to the truth of his situation, which was that he had discovered his vocation. In a creative outpouring, which Coleridge fostered but did not cause, Wordsworth had written a tragedy, a fine blank-verse narrative, *The Ruined Cottage*, and the poems, including *Tintern Abbey*, that made up *Lyrical Ballads* (1798). He had, most important of all, conceived of *The Recluse*, a life's work which would somehow embody all that Wordsworth believed he had learned about Nature, Man, and Society.

The Two-Part Prelude is written by a man who knows his strength and now, at last, believes that he knows why he knows it. As he traces his life back to the dawn of infancy, he sees at every stage how *all* of the elements of his childhood and youth worked together to form him as an independent, secure, and above all a creative being. Although it contains much of Wordsworth's finest and best-loved verse about the delights and terrors of childhood, this is not a poem about childhood, but about the processes that culminate in the formation of a man, one able, despite personal anxiety and anguish over social disintegration, to retain 'a more than Roman confidence' in Man's power to renew himself and progress. In the vigour of a blank verse which is not Shakespeare's, nor Milton's, but a new sound in English poetry, in the resourcefulness of its diction, and in the certainty and coherence with which it deploys its material, *The Two-Part Prelude* breathes the assurance of a poet who knows that in the 'honourable toil' of the philosophical poem that awaits him he has found his God-given vocation.

After his return to the Lake District in 1799 Wordsworth worked hard and on a broad front. He drafted a 'Prospectus' for the whole *Recluse* project, which is now recognised as one of the key documents of English Romanticism. The second edition of *Lyrical Ballads* in 1800, which carried his name on the title page, offered such characteristic work of his genius as *Michael* and *The Brothers*, and many more lyrics, such as *Resolution and Independence* and 'I wandered lonely as a cloud', followed in a lyrical outpouring in 1802. A longish celebration of *Home at Grasmere* was drafted as a start on the first book of *The Recluse* and he returned to further struggles with *The Ruined Cottage*, a philosophical-cum-narrative poem which seemed destined for a place in the big project. Reviewers started to take notice, so that by 1803 the previously unknown poet had the beginnings of a reputation.

If we add to this potted account of Wordsworth's activities after 1799 the fact that he married in 1802 and soon began a family, it becomes clear that when he took up the autobiographical poem again in 1803 it was from a different stand-point from that of 1799. Then Wordsworth had signalled the end of his wandering years with a declaration of hope and a welcome to the unknown. Now he knew that his hope had been justified and that his decision to return to his native mountains had been the right one. *The Recluse* (it was true) had not been written, but material towards it was in process and much else had been composed and published. As he shaped his poem, therefore, through various conceptions to the thirteen-book form completed in 1805, he presented his past life in accordance with three convictions. The first is that although he did not see it in the confused and uncertain course of his early manhood, he was through all experiences 'a chosen son' working out his destiny. The second is that his retired life of imaginative creation was actually a more truly valuable life than that of academic competition or political activism. And the third is that all of his experiences − in the Lakes, in London, and in France − had fitted him to become not a 'Nature poet' in the limited sense of that phrase, but a celebrant of Man and of his divine potential. In *The Prelude* of 1805 Wordsworth became the first poet in the English language to attempt, in Robert Rehder's perceptive words, 'to take full possession of his own life' (*Wordsworth and the Beginnings of Modern Poetry*, p. 43).

The biographical problem

The above section has suggested that knowledge of the biographical matrix of the poem can help a reader appreciate the way in which its structure is shaped to project a certain self-image — a topic which will be explored further in chapter 3. But there is another feature of the poem, which is evident on any close reading of it, which is also illuminated if we consider one particular aspect of *The Prelude*. The poem is an autobiography. The problem is not, however, that the poem is autobiographical, but that it is doubly so. Viewed as a chronological narrative, the poem is a record of Wordsworth's life up to the point at which he conceived *The Recluse* in 1798. It gives an account of the growth of the poet's mind, casting right back to the infant running about out of doors, 'A naked savage, in the thunder-shower', and ending with an evocation of the *annus mirabilis* of 1798, in which the most famous of the *Lyrical Ballads* were written by Coleridge and Wordsworth, two poets who now recognised their destiny to be 'Prophets of Nature' (XIII, 442). Highly selective and shaped though the materials of the poem are, the time-span across which they are presented is from 1770, the year of Wordsworth's birth, to 1798. But while the poem describes and narrates the years 1770–98 it also, less obviously, inscribes the years 1799–1805 during which it was composed. That it does so was inevitable, for not only was Wordsworth seeking to recall his formative years from a stand-point in the present, he also took five years over his task. To put it simply: the Wordsworth who began *The Prelude* was not the Wordsworth who finished it, and his awareness of that fact is one of the shaping powers of the poem.

For Wordsworth 1799–1805 was a period of rapid intellectual and poetic development and change. As he looked back over his life to 1798, therefore, during the years in which *The Prelude* was being composed, he did so not as one whose mind is made up but as one continually invigorated and challenged by new ideas and concepts. One record of his intellectual growth is the varied poetry and prose written in the period 1799–1805. The other is *The Prelude*. The two bodies of work interpenetrate, the prose and lyric poetry acting as an interpretative gloss on *The Prelude* and that poem in turn casting light on them.

Examples are needed to make this difficult point clear. The first can focus on the concept of the Imagination. Throughout *The Prelude* the poet traces the growth of the creative Imagination, declaring in Book XIII, 167–70, that this power,

> which in truth
> Is but another name for absolute strength
> And clearest insight, amplitude of mind,
> And reason in her most exalted mood

has been both the originating energy and the subject matter of the whole poem. During his formative years, however, with which the poem is ostensibly concerned, nowhere in his poems, letters, or discursive prose, does Wordsworth refer to Imagination in these exalted terms. But the critical-theoretical Preface to *Lyrical Ballads* (written in 1800 and greatly developed for the edition of 1802) employs a sophisticated vocabulary for discussing Imagination and makes claims for poetry as a mode of philosophic writing whose object is Truth, which reveal just how deeply engaged Wordsworth is in pondering this most important of Romantic concepts. In this instance, as he shapes his retrospective account of his own development, Wordsworth uses formulations and models which were foreign to him *then* (1770–98) but which are engrossing him *now* (1799–1805).

A second, very striking example. In the *Two-Part Prelude* two particularly powerful memories had been described as 'spots of time' which in a mysterious way retained a power to nourish the poet's mind. For the 1805 poem these passages were removed from the sequence of descriptions of childhood experiences and placed in Book XI at the climax of Wordsworth's testimony to all of those factors which had saved him from error and 'maintained a saving intercourse' with his 'true self'. The power of the poetry itself seems to bear witness to the importance of these particular memories and to confirm that they should stand at a climactic moment of affirmation in the poem. (There is further discussion of these passages in chapter 3.) But Wordsworth has not just copied out again the lines he had written for the *Two-Part Prelude*. In between the two 'spots of time' he has inserted a personal confession which cuts across the confident declaration that moments of memory such as these retain their power with 'distinct preeminence'. They do, but the poet also says:

> The days gone by
> Come back upon me from the dawn almost
> Of life; the hiding places of my power
> Seem open, I approach, and then they close;
> I see by glimpses now, when age comes on
> May scarcely see at all.

(XI, 333–8)

In these poignant lines the poet of 1804 interrupts the sequence in which he has been describing his spiritual crisis and redemption of 1795–7, revealing an anxious awareness that even as he struggles to 'enshrine the spirit of the past' in poetry, access to the sources of his power is becoming more uncertain. For a moment the text is unignorably a text both of past history *and* present consciousness. A reader of *The Prelude* can sense the tension in the verse and read on. But for a fuller understanding of the anxiety disclosed in the confessional passage and evidence that it was not a momentary emotion but a deep concern of Wordsworth's at this time, the reader must turn to other poems of 1802–4, most notably to *Resolution and Independence* and the *Ode: Intimations of Immortality*.

One final example will suffice. In 1803 Wordsworth joined the Ambleside militia, ready to fight for his country should the expected invasion by the French take place. His sister smiled at his ardour, but this was no empty gesture. Donning uniform was all of a piece with the recent composition of a series of nationalistic but not jingoistic sonnets, in which he had revealed how committed he was to the survival of British liberty – 'Earth's best hopes rest all with Thee!' Wordsworth had become and publicly declared himself a staunch patriot. When he at last approached, in 1804, that part of his autobiographical record which was to deal with his commitment to the ideals of the French Revolution and his disillusion with the revolution's course, he was therefore looking back from a very changed political viewpoint from the one of the tormented twenty-three-year-old, who had sat in a village church praying for victory, not for his country but for its enemy, and feeding his imagination on the day of vengeance yet to come. But Wordsworth's account of this period of commitment and subsequent disillusion (roughly 1791–6) is neither an act of self-exculpation, nor, on the other hand, an unqualified disavowal of his earlier self. Unlike Coleridge and Southey who tried to repudiate their radical past, Wordsworth the militiaman still claims kin with the fervent humanitarian, whose 'heart was all / Given to the people, and [whose] love was theirs'. While acknowledging error, and evoking it with imaginative power that suggests just how strong its hold on him once had been, Wordsworth insists that even in error there was that which was productive of good. The result is a section of *The Prelude* that calls for the most attentive reading. Books IX and X are often skimmed because they are about politics and apparently little more than a chronicle, but in fact no part of the poem is more demanding. In these books most clearly of all the verse registers the effort involved in re-invoking and analysing past emotion without effacing it, the struggle of being true to the past *and* to the present.

The poem to Coleridge

This introduction has highlighted elements in the compositional history of *The Prelude* which substantially affect how

it presents itself to readers today. One further, very striking feature needs to be discussed, namely, that this is a
poem addressed to a particular historical person. When the
thirteen-book version was completed in 1805, two fair-copy
manuscripts were prepared. On the title page of one of them,
in ornate calligraphy, stand the words: 'Poem / Title not yet
fixed upon / by / William Wordsworth / Addressed to / S.
T. Coleridge'. And this is how the poem was known in the
Wordsworth circle: it was 'the poem to Coleridge'.

That the poem was addressed to a named person was not,
of course, anything new in literary history. Poets had always
dedicated their works to patrons or friends and in some cases
the impact of the relationship of poet and addressee extends
beyond a formal dedicatory epistle into the body of the work
itself. Dante's sense of the living presence of Cavalcanti
informs *La Vita Nuova*. Spenser's consciousness of his relationship to, but not with, Queen Elizabeth I, permeates *The
Faerie Queene*.

What is new about *The Prelude* is the size of the addressee's
role and the degree of historical specificity with which it is
established. Throughout the poem Wordsworth speaks directly
to Coleridge in momentary interjections, such as 'Ah, need
I say dear friend', or 'Thus from an early age, O friend'.
Examples (not a complete list) are IV, 340; VI, 681; VII, 13;
VIII, 472; VIII, 860; IX, 249; X, 466; X, 880; XI, 41.
Coleridge is thus absent, yet ever-present. In *Tintern Abbey*
the fiction is that Dorothy Wordsworth is standing at the
poet's side. When he addresses his 'dear, dear sister', his
attention shifts from the landscape to the human being gazing
at it with him. Sara Coleridge darts a look of mild reproof at
her husband in *The Eolian Harp* – she is there with him. The
absent friends of *This Lime-Tree Bower* have left Coleridge
only moments before and, despite the plaintive self-pity of the
opening lines, will soon be back. But Coleridge is absent from
The Prelude, and his absence is made the more apparent by
the fact that he is so continuously invoked, as if by words of
endearment, and repetition of his name, Wordsworth might
conjure his presence.

Elsewhere, however, Coleridge is addressed not just as the poem's reader/auditor, but as its subject; that is, Coleridge's relation to the poem or to the poet, or his own situation, or his past, become the focus. Examples are I, 645–63; II, 215–36; II, 466–84; III, 314–28; VI, 246–330; X, 940–1038; XI, 389–95; XII, 356–65; XIII, 246–70; XIII, 370–452. In these passages, some of which are quite long, Wordsworth addresses, so to speak, not Coleridge but the question of Coleridge.

The brief interjections, 'Ah, dear friend . . .' fix Coleridge in an unchanging role. He is always the poet's ideal reader, the one who will understand. With the major addresses, on the other hand, it is quite different. Coleridge remains the ideal reader, but as the poem progresses it is noticeable that the poet's relationship to him changes markedly. Coleridge's status in relation to the ongoing composition is transformed.

In the opening books of *The Prelude* Coleridge is treated both as an originating first cause and as a kindly monitor. The poem is to be written to give Coleridge 'better knowledge how the heart was framed / Of him thou lovest', but should it fail, the poet knows he need not 'dread . . . Harsh judgements' (I, 656–8). Coleridge, 'one / The most intense of Nature's worshippers' (II, 476–7), is imaged as a traveller who has reached the 'self-same bourne' as the poet, but 'by different roads' (II, 468–9). Shaped by different experiences, Coleridge has gone before. He is one to whom 'unblinded by these outward shows / The unity of all has been revealed' (II, 225–6). Wordsworth thus offers his own tentative gropings towards self-understanding to a wise precursor, one 'More deeply read in [his] own thoughts' (II, 216).

As the poem proceeds, the implied relationship between the two poets changes. Musing on their Cambridge years, for example, Wordsworth plays with a fancy that had he known Coleridge then, his 'maturer age / And temperature less willing to be moved / [His] calmer habits, and more steady voice' (VI, 321–3) might have prevented the wreck of his university career. Wordsworth's strong self-assessment appears still more strikingly at X, 940–1038. After a long account of how he fell into error and despair, from which he was restored by various agencies to his 'true self' (X, 915), Wordsworth addresses the sick Coleridge who has fled south in search of health. The tone of the passage is not in the least condescending, but it is unquestionably the voice of one who feels strong, sane, and whole. At a 'heavy time of change for all mankind' (X, 985), when England remains the 'last spot of earth where Freedom now / Stands single in her only sanctuary' (X, 981–2), Coleridge is wandering in degenerate Sicily, a broken man, 'a captive pining for his home' (X, 1038). Wishing health upon him — which means much more than just relief from physical ailments — Wordsworth is wishing to restore Coleridge as he was at the beginning of the poem.

This yearning is nowhere more apparent than in *The Prelude*'s close, where the relative position the two poets had at the beginning of the poem is completely reversed. Then Wordsworth has looked to Coleridge as a monitor, who, both by example and loving support, would assist him in his life's work — ultimately *The Recluse*. Now at the end of *The Prelude* it is Wordsworth who is encouraging and implicitly admonishing Coleridge. By looking back to the gladness of the summer of 1798 and by invoking poetic achievement in *The Ancient Mariner* and *Christabel* which Coleridge had never since matched, Wordsworth reminds Coleridge that once they had conceived of themselves as 'joint labourers' on a holy mission. Their task, *The Prelude* asserts in conclusion, remains. And what Wordsworth can give Coleridge by way of encouragement is nothing less than *The Prelude* itself: 'this offering of my love' (XIII, 427).

The tender lines in which this promise is made lead us to the appropriate conclusion to this introduction, to the moment when Coleridge received 'his' poem.

Coleridge returned to England in 1806, having been abroad since mid – 1804, and late in the year he joined the anxiously expectant Wordsworths in Leicestershire. On successive evenings over the turn of the year Wordsworth read out *The Prelude*. They must have been amongst the most poignant evenings in English literary history. Before Coleridge had set

sail for the Mediterranean barely contained tensions had ir-
reversibly damaged the togetherness of the Alfoxden year,
but now all of the circle desperately hoped that it might be
renewed. *The Prelude* was designed in part to restore the two
poets to their former intimacy. And for a while it seemed to
have succeeded. On the night of Wordsworth's final reading,
Coleridge composed much of his last substantial poem, *To
William Wordsworth* (printed pp. 542–5 in 'The Norton
Prelude'). This, the first recorded critical response to the
poem, is a generous, lofty-toned tribute to Wordsworth, now
firmly placed in Coleridge's judgement 'in the Choir / Of
ever-enduring Men'. In fact, however, the two moved in-
exorably further apart. *To William Wordsworth*, like the
closing lines of *The Prelude* itself, remains a moving
testimony, but the pathos of both stems from our knowledge
that they mark the end, not the renewal, of each poet's power
to inspire the other.

Chapter 2

The Verse

Introduction

The Prelude is a *long poem*. The difficulties presented by the first of these two words are formidable. There is the difficulty of length pure and simple. Reading *The Prelude* with concentration would take some days and it is doubtful whether anyone reaching the end for the first time would remember much of the early books in any detail, if at all. But it is not just a matter of length by line-count. The length of *The Prelude* confuses in a way that that of other nineteenth-century long poems does not. *Don Juan, The Ring and the Book, The Idylls of the King*, all make demands of a reader's perseverance and require reading skills which few twentieth-century readers are used to exercise on poetry, but they do not confuse. However complex they are in detail, however multi-layered and challenging the verse itself, each of these poems proceeds by making its architecture ever more apparent. The first canto or book suggests a shape to be unfolded, and an approach to the subject matter, which are not countermanded by what follows.

How different *The Prelude*. Abashed by the length of his recently completed poem, Wordsworth confessed to Sir George Beaumont that it was 'a thing unprecedented in Literary history that a man should talk so much about himself' (1 May 1805), but what a reader fresh to the poem might want to stress is not the length but the indiscipline it licenses. Personal narrative which points up chronology is juxtaposed with narrative which gives no answer to the questions, 'when did this incident take place relative to that?' or 'how often did this experience occur?' Two mountain ascents – Snowdon and the Alps – are separated by half the length of the poem. There must be a structural significance, but what? Book V claims to be about books, but isn't. What exactly is the content of Book XII, or in which Books do the major addresses to Coleridge appear? Feelings of guilty apprehension often arise when these questions are asked. It is, simply, difficult to remember the *structure* of a poem whose length seems not to be the instrument of elucidation or clarification.

Only repeated explorations of the whole poem can make a reader easy with its terrain, but help can be found in the books listed in the guide to further reading, pp. 108–10 and, I hope, in the next chapters.

The second word of the phrase 'long poem' also causes difficulties, but here it is not possible to refer readers to much helpful commentary. That medium and content are, fundamentally, indissoluble, especially in poetry, is a given of literary criticism, but in practice it is hard to honour this truth. Wordsworth insisted that poetry was *art*, success in which demanded skills and application 'which can proceed from nothing but practice' (24 September 1827). When offered poems for criticism his invariable response was to comment on the technicalities of the verse form, admitting on one occasion that he inclined to pernicketiness: 'my ear is susceptible of the clashing of sounds almost to disease'. Most critics, however, do not follow Wordsworth's lead. Little attention has been paid to *The Prelude*'s medium, the blank verse. With much commentary, in fact, it is only from quotations that one can tell that the poem is not in rhymed couplets or Spenserian stanzas.

It is not difficult to see why this should be so. First: medium and content are obviously indissoluble in lyrics by, for example, Marvell or Keats or Hopkins, but less obviously so in a poem made up of thousands of lines of blank verse. To extract for discussion the content of *The Garden*, or *Ode to a Nightingale*, or *The Windhover*, that is, to paraphrase what the poem is 'about', does violence to what the poem is. But though in theory this must also be true for *The Prelude*, we cannot in fact behave as if it is. Clearly it is possible to

inspect the content of Book VIII, for example, without constant reference to the verse medium, whereas a discussion of
Ode to a Nightingale that did not focus on rhythm, rhyme,
and stanza formation would not be a literary discussion at all.

Second: there is the sheer difficulty of saying anything
about a medium as elusive as blank verse. In his highly
influential *Conjectures on Original Composition* (1759)
Edward Young declared, 'what we mean by blank verse is,
verse unfallen, uncurst; verse reclaimed, reinthroned in the
true language of the gods; who never thundered, nor suffered
their Homer to thunder, in rhyme', but it is notable that he
defines the form through negatives. It is easier to say what
blank verse is not than to demonstrate what its properties and
powers are. This chapter will fail to give a satisfactory
account of Wordsworth's blank verse (even as an introduction), as all other attempts have done.

Third: there is the sense that it is somehow inappropriate
to talk about Wordsworth as a verse technician. Matthew
Arnold's assertion (in the Preface to his selection *Poems of
Wordsworth*, 1879) that 'Wordsworth's poetry, when he is at
his best, is inevitable, as inevitable as Nature herself. It might
seem that Nature not only gave him the matter for his poem,
but wrote the poem for him. He has no style', engages with
a truth. A poem which celebrates freedom in its opening lines,
which constantly opposes formal education to Nature's care,
and which directly privileges sane, deep, personally intuitive
response over 'rules of mimic art transferred / To things
above all art' (XI, 154–5), seems to direct attention away
from art as such. At key moments there is always silence,
'when the light of sense / Goes out in flashes that have shown
to us / The invisible world' (VI, 534–6), and at such moments
the poet hymns experience beyond words. Just as the child
of the *Ode: Intimations*, who 'readst the eternal deep' is
'deaf and silent', so the poet in *The Prelude* attains a state
beyond utterance when experience of the transcendental
realm is at its most intense. Of course Wordsworth is as lock-
ed as any poet in what Eliot called 'the intolerable wrestle /
With words and meanings', but at its most memorable the

verse affirms a state of pure being, when the tongue is still. As a response to this poetry Arnold's comment makes sense. Justifying his statement that he only cared for religious poetry, Wordsworth explained, 'it is the imaginative only, viz., that which is conversant [with], or turns upon infinity, that powerfully affects me . . . those passages where things are lost in each other, and limits vanish, and aspirations are raised' (21 January 1824). In the face of such loftiness, it hardly seems appropriate (Arnold seems to suggest) to talk about 'style'.

Wordsworth's first and best critic, Coleridge, however, saw the matter differently. To him Wordsworth's style was unignorably self-advertising. Reading the 'There was a boy' passage (V, 389–413) for the first time, Coleridge acknowledged the 'affecting impression' left by the whole, but mentioned specifically the closing lines,

> Its woods, and that uncertain heaven, received
> Into the bosom of the steady lake.

'I should have recognised [them] anywhere; and had I met these lines running wild in the deserts of Arabia, I should have instantly screamed out "Wordsworth!" ' (letter, 10 December 1798).

This is very interesting. When Coleridge did first meet these lines, not in the deserts of Arabia but in snow-covered Germany in 1798, Wordsworth had not written a lot of non-dramatic blank verse, yet Coleridge senses that he is already producing something with a characteristic identity. And trying to account for the flash of recognition that delights him, Coleridge just quotes, as Arnold was to do later, when he isolated a single line from *Michael*

> And never lifted up a single stone

as a touchstone of Wordsworthian simplicity and of great poetry.

In formulating his response in terms of instant recognition Coleridge was, as so often, suggestively right. Wordsworth's blank verse was his own. It was not, of course, a spontaneous

birth. Milton (*Paradise Lost*, 1667) begat it; A
(*Pleasures of Imagination*, 1744) and Cowper (*Th
1785) nurtured it. But in *The Prelude* Wordsworth br
of his great progenitor, free enough, as Akenside and Cowper
never were, to be Miltonic when strategy demanded, without
fear of losing his identity. Any reader familiar with *Paradise
Lost* and *The Idylls of the King* would immediately recognise
twenty lines from *The Prelude* as different from Milton's or
Tennyson's blank verse, even though explaining why might
prove taxing.

What follows is an introductory exploration of Wordsworth's distinctive voice. It is not a comprehensive study —
that much-to-be-desired book still waits to be written — but
a series of observations designed to alert readers to some of
the more striking features of the verse.

Variety

A major contribution of Coleridge and Wordsworth to
English lyric poetry is the 'Conversation Poem', an apparently free-flowing, personal meditation, centred on or
addressed to someone very dear to the poet. Such a definition
encompasses *The Prelude*. The poem is a laying bare of
the self to those most lovingly concerned with that self,
Coleridge, Dorothy, and Mary Wordsworth. But although
The Prelude is undoubtedly an outgrowth of *Frost at Midnight* and *Tintern Abbey*, it is not just an engorged Conversation Poem. The Conversation Poems operate within limited
parameters of manner and tone, striving to create the impression of an extempore meditation. *The Prelude*, on the contrary, exploits diversity of manner and tone (within the
generous overall limitations imposed by the blank verse) for
the multiple purposes of the long poem. Since this book is too
short for ample quotation, the reader must use the list that
follows with the text of the poem in hand as a pointer to some
of *The Prelude*'s variety.

The most immediately attractive poetry, and therefore the
most anthologised, is that which dwells on intense experiences

of pleasure or fear in the poet's childhood. For example:

> All shod with steel
> We hissed along the polished ice in games
> Confederate, imitative of the chace
> And woodland pleasures, the resounding horn,
> The pack loud bellowing, and the hunted hare.
> So through the darkness and the cold we flew,
> And not a voice was idle. With the din,
> Meanwhile, the precipices rang aloud;
> The leafless trees and every icy crag
> Tinkled like iron; while the distant hills
> Into the tumult sent an alien sound
> Of melancholy, not unnoticed; while the stars,
> Eastward, were sparkling clear, and in the west
> The orange sky of evening died away.
>
> (I, 460–73)

Other examples are I, 372–426 ('The Stolen Boat'), I, 333–50 ('Skating'), II, 99–144 ('Furness Abbey Excursion'), II, 145–80 ('Boating on Windermere'), V, 389–413 ('The Winander Boy'), XI, 278–315 ('Woman on Penrith Beacon'), XI, 344–88 ('Waiting for the Horses'). Each of these passages evokes through suggestive detail a specific Lake District scene and moves to a climax in which the interpenetration of the boy's whole being with the natural phenomena is total. It is fair to say that such poetry moves readers not only because it evokes what everyone remembers, 'the eagerness of infantine desire' (II, 26), but also because it activates one's own store of images. A visit to the Lake District is not a prerequisite for responding to this poetry, but it certainly helps to have seen a mountain against massing clouds or to have sat at water-level beside a dead still lake.

Much of the verse, by contrast, is very 'literary', that is, it calls upon an awareness of poetic register that can only come from knowledge of literary tradition. Throughout Book III, for example, Wordsworth seems to have difficulty in focussing on the specifics of his Cambridge experience and eventually employs sustained personification to suggest that the university was peopled with types:

And here was Labour, his own Bond-slave; Hope
That never set the pains against the prize;
Idleness, halting with his weary clog;
And poor misguided Shame, and witless Fear,
And simple Pleasure, foraging for Death;
Honour misplaced, and Dignity astray;
Feuds, factions, flatteries, Enmity and Guile,
Murmuring Submission and bald Government
(The idol weak as the idolator)
And Decency and Custom starving Truth
And blind Authority beating with his staff
The child that might have led him; Emptiness
Followed as of good omen, and meek Worth
Left to itself unheard of and unknown.

(III, 630–43)

In Book VII the type of the fashionable preacher appears in
a satiric sketch that looks back to Cowper, even to Pope and
Dryden:

There have I seen a comely bachelor,
Fresh from a toilette of two hours, ascend
The pulpit, with seraphic glance look up,
And in a tone elaborately low
Beginning, lead his voice through many a maze
A minuet course, and, winding up his mouth
From time to time into an orifice
Most delicate, a lurking eyelet, small
And only not invisible, again
Open it out, diffusing thence a smile
Of rapt irradiation exquisite.

(VII, 547–57)

The children's card-game in Book I, 541–62, becomes,
through brief but telling use of the mock-heroic, a battle with

Queens, gleaming through their splendour's last decay;
And monarchs, surly at the wrongs sustained
By royal visages.

In Book VIII, 711–41, Wordsworth appropriates a rhetorical
figure from Classical and Miltonic epic, the heroic simile,
beginning, 'As when a traveller . . .', to convey the impact

on his imagination made by the multitudinousness of London, a type of figure also employed at IV, 247–64, 'As one who hangs . . .'. On numerous occasions Wordsworth uses the figure of apostrophe. The narrative or discursive flow pauses, as the poet addresses a person or a single aspect of his subject matter. Notable examples are X, 940–1038 (the apostrophe to Coleridge), and VI, 525–48 (the address to Imagination).

At such moments as these the verse calls attention to itself as art. The tone of a passage may be misjudged if the reader does not have some acquaintance, however slight, with the genres and rhetorical figures deployed. At other moments, however, the verse calls for a more decisively 'literary' reading. In Book IX, 38–82 Wordsworth describes how on his return to Paris at the end of 1792 his imagination was wrought up by the dread he sensed everywhere

> Until I seemed to hear a voice that cried
> To the whole city, 'Sleep no more!'

No reader is likely to miss the signalled quotation from *Macbeth* or the appropriateness of an allusion to another text which dramatises the result of power unleashed. Other more significant allusions in *The Prelude*, however, are more subdued. In Book III, 178–83, for example, Wordsworth declares:

> O heavens, how awful is the might of souls
> And what they do within themselves while yet
> The yoke of earth is new to them, the world
> Nothing but a wild field where they were sown.
> This is in truth heroic argument,
> And genuine prowess.

This is clearly an important statement of Wordsworth's theme, but its significance is emphasised when one registers that 'heroic argument, / And genuine prowess' echoes in order to challenge and displace two declarations by Milton of the importance of *his* theme in *Paradise Lost* (I, 24; IX, 28–9).

The opening to *The Prelude* is a fabric of allusion.

Rhapsodising on his freedom, the poet images himself as like the Israelites, released 'from a house of bondage' (*Prelude*, I, 6–7; Exodus 13:3) – the Israelites were seeking the Promised Land – and then declares 'The earth is all before me . . .' (15). The evocation of the beautiful closing lines of *Paradise Lost* opens out the grandeur of Wordsworth's sense of liberty:

> Some natural tears they dropped, but wiped them soon;
> The world was all before them, where to choose
> Their place of rest, and providence their guide:
> They hand in hand, with wandering steps and slow,
> Through Eden took their solitary way.

Adam and Eve hesitantly step out of Paradise into a fallen world, Providence their guide. Wordsworth opens his poem where Milton ends, with the fully human being at large in the world. But here the 'gentle breeze' itself brings 'blessing', and as for providence, the poet is confident that

> should the guide I chuse
> Be nothing better than a wandering cloud
> I cannot miss my way.

(17–19)

Much of the verse of *The Prelude* serves a narrative function, that is, it marks the passing of time and moves the poet from place to place. But the chronicle aspect of the poem is markedly subdued. Wordsworth dramatises and highlights significant experiences only, turning back on himself and collapsing chronology bewilderingly. At two points in the poem, however, he foregrounds narrative as narrative, introducing into his text other fully-shaped stories, 'The Matron's Tale' of Lake District shepherd life at VIII, 222–311 and 'Vaudracour and Julia', a tale of the clash of love and family duties in pre-Revolutionary France, at IX, 556–935.

Much of the verse of *The Prelude* is also meditative and reflective. The most sustained, difficult, and important such passage at XIII, 66–119, actually announces itself as a 'meditation'. Similarly, a discussion of the picturesque at XI, 137–94, suggests that, difficult though the verse is, 'abstruser argument' would be needed for full consideration of the topic. Most of the reflective passages, however, do not signal their significance in this way. They are allowed to rise seemingly naturally from the experience which is their origin.

Finally, it has to be admitted that much of the verse is unexcitingly functional — not sensuously concrete, not allusive, not rhetorically significant, not intellectually demanding. It is the staple medium of the poem:

> My present theme
> Is to retrace the way that led me on
> Through Nature to the love of human-kind;
> Nor could I with such object overlook
> The influence of this power which turned itself
> Instinctively to human passions, things
> Least understood — of this adulterate power,
> For so it may be called, and without wrong,
> When with that first compared. Yet in the midst
> Of these vagaries . . .

(VIII, 586–95)

Such verse is unmemorable and it would never win space in an anthology. Any claims made for it at all are going to sound like special pleading. But what can be said with confidence is that no long and varied poem in blank verse can be shaped without it and that even major poets such as Milton, Browning and Tennyson (ignoring Wordsworth's predecessors in reflective verse, Cowper and Akenside), have difficulty in finding a voice for and sustaining interest in their middle style.

Rhythm and syntax

In 1798 Wordsworth told the German poet Klopstock that in his view 'harmonious verse . . . consisted (the English iambic blank verse above all) in the apt arrangement of pauses and cadences and the sweep of whole paragraphs . . . and not in the even flow, much less in the prominence or antithetic vigour, of single lines' (Coleridge's report). Wordsworth might have recited the recollection of birds'-nesting 'on the lonesome peaks', which he was currently working on:

> Nor less in springtime, when on southern banks
> The shining sun had from her knot of leaves

Decoyed the primrose flower, and when the vales
And woods were warm, was I a plunderer then
In the high places, on the lonesome peaks,
Where'er among the mountains and the winds
The mother-bird had built her lodge. Though mean
My object and inglorious, yet the end
Was not ignoble. Oh, when I have hung
Above the raven's nest, by knots of grass
And half-inch fissures in the slippery rock
But ill sustained, and almost, as it seemed,
Suspended by the blast which blew amain,
Shouldering the naked crag, oh, at that time
While on the perilous ridge I hung alone,
With what strange utterance did the loud dry wind
Blow through my ears; the sky seemed not a sky
Of earth, and with what motion moved the clouds!

(I, 333–50)

The latter part of this passage, from 'Oh, when . . .' is one
sentence. The 'sweep' arises from the length of time and
effort it takes to speak or read it whole. And it is an effort,
for as Christopher Ricks has said in the finest discussion yet
of Wordsworth's blank verse, it 'asks that we take our time'
(*Essays in Criticism*, 1971, p. 28). The syntax of the primary,
direct statement has to be registered (Oh, when . . . oh, at that
time . . . the sky seemed . . . and with what motion . . .) at
the same time as the suspensions and modifications which
simultaneously enrich yet delay fulfilment of the sense. The
repeated 'hung' sustains the sentence, but the weight carried
is massed by participial phrases around 'sustained', 'suspended', 'shouldering'. The description of Furness Abbey in
II, 122–35 offers another splendid example of a long sentence
where clause modifying clause so impedes directness that the
whole seems to enact the boys' lingering reluctance to move
on. As Donald Davie has noted, 'this is poetry where the
syntax counts enormously, counts for nearly everything'
(*Articulate Energy*, p. 111).

But in itself not quite everything. What is notable about
Wordsworth's blank verse at its finest is that it exploits the
conjunction of what Davie terms the 'articulate energy' of
syntax, which is perceptible whether the verse is spoken or

read, with the properties of *printed* verse, which are perceptible only to the eye. 'As long as blank verse shall be printed
in lines', Wordsworth wrote, 'it will be physically impossible
to pronounce the last words or syllables of the lines with the
same indifference, as the others, i.e. not to give them an in-
tonation of one kind or an other, or to follow them with a
pause, not called out for by the passion of the subject, but by
the passion of metre merely' (letter to John Thelwall, mid-
January 1804). In the birds'-nesting passage such pauses work
against the syntax, momentarily dissolving the certainty of
meaning. Does the boy hang 'by knots of grass', as the pause
at the end of the line satisfactorily suggests? Yes, but the syntax doesn't, it appears, quite say so. He hangs above the
raven's nest, 'ill-sustained' by fissures in the rock as well as
knots of grass. The line ending, 'which blew amain', refuses
more obdurately to allow certainty: 'the blast which blew
amain / Shouldering the naked crag, oh, at that time / While
on the perilous ridge I hung alone'. Is it the wind shouldering
the crag, or the boy? Or is it both, the boy pressed hard
against the rock by the force of the blast? One final example.
In the penultimate line of the quotation the eye, registering
however briefly the pause at the end of 'the sky seemed not
a sky' absorbs one meaning which makes good sense, before,
enacting the enjambement, it absorbs another ('not a sky / Of
earth'), which makes no sense at all. Ricks puts it strikingly:
'The extraordinary vision glimpsed here, as of a calm vertigo,
is one which delights in calling up a suggestion which it then
has the power to exorcise: we are to entertain the phantasmal
unimaginability of a sky of earth − to entertain it, and then
with a wise relief to cleave to the other sense' (*Essays in
Criticism*, 1971, p. 23).

Inner and outer: prepositions

One word from the birds'-nesting passage is worth further
comment, it is such a characteristic Wordsworthian usage: the
preposition 'through'. ('*Preposition*: word governing . . .
noun or pronoun, expressing latter's relation to another

word'. *OED*) The account of the boy's exploit overall emphasises physicality and closeness to resisting Nature –
hanging from knots of grass, fingers and toes scrabbling for
half-inch fissures in the rock – but no word is more powerful
than the innocuous-looking 'through':

> With what strange utterance did the loud dry wind
> Blow through my ears . . .

Not 'in my ears', or 'on my ears', but 'through my ears', con-
veying the sense that the wind which buffets the crag and half
holds the boy up, passes as directly *through* him as it does
through a tuft of grass. Governing the relation of one word
to another, the preposition in this case relates the animate to
the inanimate, reinforcing the early *Prelude*'s repeated assertion that Nature intertwines the boy's whole being with the
'forms and images' of the phenomenal world (I, 427–41).

At the end of the 'Stolen Boat' episode (I, 372–426), the
same word functions even more strikingly. Terrified by the
dissolution of boundaries between inner and outer, between
the permanent stability of mountains and the mind's equally
stable grasp of what is and what is not real, the boy rows back
to shore and replaces the stolen boat. But his sense of the
world is not as easily restored:

>   and after I had seen
> That spectacle, for many days my brain
> Worked with a dim and undetermined sense
> Of unknown modes of being. In my thoughts
> There was a darkness – call it solitude
> Or blank desertion – no familiar shapes
> Of hourly objects, images of trees,
> Of sea or sky, no colours of green fields,
> But huge and mighty forms that do not live
> Like living men moved slowly through my mind
> By day, and were the trouble of my dreams.

'Through my mind'. The huge and mighty forms claim a
realm to move about in as capaciously three-dimensional as
the lake itself across which the mountain seemed to stride.
What is 'mind' and what is its relation to the 'outside' world?
In one way or another every philosopher from Locke onwards

had engaged with the question in the light of increasing speculation about – and some knowledge of – the physiology of the brain. Neurophysiologists are still engaged with it. In this passage a single word affirms the poet's sense that whatever its electro-chemical components may be, the mind is experienced as a place, busy in an unpreventable commerce with the so-called external world.

The lines which Coleridge declared he would recognise running wild in the deserts of Arabia offer another striking example of prepositional use. This quotation comes from the second part of the description of the boy hooting to the owls across Lake Windermere:

> And when it chanced
> That pauses of deep silence mocked his skill,
> Then sometimes in that silence, while he hung
> Listening, a gentle shock of mild surprize
> Has carried far into his heart the voice
> Of mountain torrents; or the visible scene
> Would enter unawares into his mind
> With all its solemn imagery, its rocks,
> Its woods, and that uncertain heaven, received
> Into the bosom of the steady lake.
>
> (V, 404–13)

De Quincey's comment – and he was one of the Romantic period's boldest explorers of the mind – cannot be bettered: 'This very expression "far", by which space and its infinities are attributed to the human heart, and to its capacities of re-echoing the sublimities of nature, has always struck me as with a flash of sublime revelation' (1839; in Jordan, *De Quincey as Critic*, p. 443)

To list further examples would be tedious and space precludes it. Enough has been said to alert the reader to an identifying feature of the verse. 'Under', 'in/into', 'along', 'through' – such words should be lingered on. They transmit the energy of *The Prelude*'s project. As a whole the poem is concerned with mind and its development – with perception, consciousness, imagination and reason – and with the phenomenal world of 'rocks and stones and trees'. Books which explore Wordsworth's poetry in the context of

eighteenth-century philosophy are not misguided, for it
clearly is cognate with philosophy's main concerns. But *The
Prelude* is not a contribution to eighteenth-century
philosophy as philosophy. What it does is embody in the way
that only imaginative art can do the human reality, the experienced urgency, of the great questions about the mind and
its powers, about feeling and intellect, about inner and outer,
the self and the external world. Wordsworth focusses on
experiences which elide distinctions, recalling formative
passages of life in language which integrates but does not
merge. In the verse the material world becomes palpable. And
in this linguistic activity prepositions play a vital part.

Verse as enactment

When the rhythmical pulse of blank verse is weak, it becomes
the flattest of all verse forms. The capital letter at the beginning of each new line, spaced out evenly like fencing posts,
tells us that this is verse, even if nothing else insists that the
lines must lie on the page in this way and no other. When the
rhythmical drive is strong and varied, however, blank verse is
capable of a marvellous range of effects. One of the most
powerful is its capacity for suggesting movement and energy,
sometimes thwarted energy, which seems to strain the verse in
its struggle for forward momentum towards a climax and
resolution.

Such verse is one of *The Prelude*'s strengths. At the crisis
of the 'Stolen Boat' episode (I, 372–426), Wordsworth recalls
how, as he rowed out across the lake in the moonlight,

> from behind that craggy steep, till then
> The bound of the horizon, a huge cliff,
> As if with voluntary power instinct,
> Upreared its head. I struck, and struck again,
> And, growing still in stature, the huge cliff
> Rose up between me and the stars, and still
> With measured motion, like a living thing
> Strode after me.

Here the repetitions, 'huge cliff . . . struck and struck again
. . . huge cliff', the two monosyllables beginning new lines,

'Rose', 'Strode', and the sinewy rhythm with the extra-ordinary weighting of 'Rose up between me and the stars', combine to convey not just a picture of the scene but the dynamics of it, the actual movement of the mountain, the boy's panic-stricken action, and the terror of his recognition that the further he rows away from it the bigger his pursuer becomes.

Individual responses to poetry are going to differ and the critic must be cautious, but I would suggest that most readers are likely to feel that the verse of the stolen boat episode is more than just appropriate for the subject matter, that it, to a degree, enacts the movement and the emotions that are its subject matter. (A glance at the revised passage in the 1850 *Prelude* will confirm this. Removing repetition and smoothing out the iambics, Wordsworth has dissipated the energy of the quoted lines.) Such enactment features in all of the most striking passages in *The Prelude*: the accounts of childhood pleasures in Books I and II; 'The Winander Boy' (V, 389–413); 'The Crossing of the Alps', especially VI, 543–72; the 'Spots of Time' (XI, 278–315, 344–88); 'The Climbing of Snowdon' (XIII, 1–66). What is common to all these passages is that physical activity combines with intense emotional activity, and that a rendering of the actual scene, in its mundane corporeality, is the ground of the release of the emotional and imaginative power which is the core of the event.

These passages, often praised as 'sensuous' or 'concrete' poetry, are rightly known as the high-points of *The Prelude*. The verse of enactment, however, also functions at a key moment in the poem, when none of the features listed above are present, and the quality of this verse has not had its due.

In Book X Wordsworth gives an account of his mental state after his return home from France at the end of 1792, through a loose chronicle of events punctuated by passages of analysis. It is a story of hopes raised, then dashed, of blows absorbed, and, increasingly, of confusion which the poet compounds by his chosen method of dispelling it. Bewildered by political controversy, he enters more energetically into controversy, determined to dissect, with 'knife in hand',

the 'living body of society / Even to the heart' (872–6). The
crisis of this process is:

> Thus I fared,
> Dragging all passions, notions, shapes of faith,
> Like culprits to the bar, suspiciously
> Calling the mind to establish in plain day
> Her titles and her honours, now believing,
> Now disbelieving, endlessly perplexed
> With impulse, motive, right and wrong, the ground
> Of moral obligation — what the rule,
> And what the sanction — till, demanding proof,
> And seeking it in everything, I lost
> All feeling of conviction, and, in fine,
> Sick, wearied out with contrarieties,
> Yielded up moral questions in despair,
> And for my future studies, as the sole
> Employment of the inquiring faculty,
> Turned towards mathematics, and their clear
> And solid evidence.
>
> (X, 888–904)

Quite as strikingly as the poetry of concrete evocation, this
passage enacts the crisis it describes. For full effect it needs
to be read out loud. The idea of a tribunal, in which the poet
is both judge and accused, is vividly conveyed through the image of the abstractions 'passions, notions, shapes of faith', as
'culprits' dragged to the bar, when the mind is called upon
like a hapless aristocrat to demonstrate her right to titles of
honour. But especially important work is done through the
rhythm which opposes believing to disbelieving, sub-divides
the ground of moral obligation, and rises to a climax, at the
end of the line, in the demand for *proof*, only to register the
futility of the demand in the exhausted 'wearied out with
contrarieties'.

There is nothing concrete about this passage or the verse
that surrounds it. Wordsworth does not reveal where he was,
what he was reading, what he was discussing or with whom,
or what the date was. At the most important crisis in its subject's personal history, *The Prelude* yields, biographically,
nothing. What this magnificent verse does do, however, is
record that from unspecific causes and in unspecific ways the

poet was tormented and in lines that suggest the power of misdirected energy, it enacts the agony of a man who, probing the living body of society, was actually using the knife against himself. And this is all that the reader needs to know and to feel. What pamphlets Wordsworth read, or with whom he discussed them, are unimportant compared with what the poet remembers was the nature of his mental turmoil.

The language of thought

The 'moral questions' passage records the crisis in Wordsworth's intellectual development. It is a crisis of thought. But in his recollection of this mental nadir the poet does not attempt to convey thought itself. As I have said, the passage enacts the torment of ideological conflict, but it is impossible to be specific, as biographers and commentators have found, about exactly what thoughts were competing for mastery. All Wordsworth says is that in the last phase before his despair, he was 'Misguiding and misguided', because his reasonings were 'false / From the beginning'. Elsewhere in the poem, however, the verse does convey thought. In fact, reflection and meditation constitute a large part of *The Prelude* and as it is such verse that the modern reader is likely to find most alien, this section on Wordsworth's blank verse ought to conclude with some words about it.

Uncertainty about *The Prelude*'s meditative verse (which can become a real fear of it) is partly a result of unfamiliarity with the genre. Readers of Yeats and Eliot, Dylan Thomas, Plath, or Heaney, are prepared for poetry to be intensely thoughtful in very differing ways, but they do not expect it to expound ideas over sometimes hundreds of lines. Eighteenth-century readers did. A way of preparing oneself for *The Prelude* would be to read *Paradise Lost*, Pope's *Essay on Man*, Young's *Night Thoughts*, Akenside's *Pleasures of Imagination*, Cowper's *The Task* and Coleridge's *Religious Musings*.

Even supposing a reader could undertake this course of study, however, the meditative verse of *The Prelude* is still likely to cause problems if it is approached timorously and with wrong expectations. Approaching untimorously does not mean charging on through the meditative miasma until the poet stops thinking and gets on with narrating or describing. *The Prelude* is intellectually demanding. The meditative verse does call for slow, careful reading. But two points might be made to encourage an untimorous approach.

First. There is no 'key' to the meditative verse of *The Prelude*. Faced with a long exposition of a state in the poet's intellectual growth, which deploys unfamiliar vocabulary, a reader may be tempted to look outside the poem for explanation, as if Wordsworth were a second-rate philosopher whose ideas benefit from glosses from a first-rate one. This is, I suggest, a mistake. Engagement with the poem may lead the student, after many readings, to Locke or Hartley, to Berkeley or to Kant, but the process of discovery must be in that order. Student guides and even more scholarly books on 'background', which provide a summary statement of Wordsworth's intellectual position, are tempting, but should be resisted. For the most helpful commentary on one passage of *The Prelude* is another passage from the poem itself.

Take, for example, the apostrophe which follows the 'Stolen Boat' episode (I, 427–40).

> Wisdom and spirit of the universe,
> Thou soul that art the eternity of thought,
> That giv'st to forms and images a breath
> And everlasting motion – not in vain,
> By day or star-light, thus from my first dawn
> Of childhood didst thou intertwine for me
> The passions that build up our human soul,
> Not with the mean and vulgar works of man,
> But with high objects, with enduring things,
> With life and Nature, purifying thus
> The elements of feeling and of thought,
> And sanctifying by such discipline
> Both pain and fear, until we recognise
> A grandeur in the beatings of the heart.

One word here, 'vulgar', has shifted in meaning since the eighteenth century and recourse to the dictionary is required.

But scanning reference books on eighteenth-century philosophy for entries on 'soul', 'spirit', 'forms', 'images', 'motion', is not the way into the unfamiliar concepts of this passage. Ultimately more productive will be the slower process of noting each succeeding use of these and similar words and interrogation of meanings as they arise in differing contexts. Only a reader very familiar with how Wordsworth uses certain words and concepts, in the specific context of his poetry, can gain anything useful for appreciation of *The Prelude* from studying how, say, Locke uses them in a quite different discourse.

Second. The meditative verse should not be approached as if it were a *précis* question in an English Language examination, even less as a test in logic. It is not versification of a pre-existing statement, which it is the reader's task to draw out cleanly, nor is it a syllogistic argument which just happens to be laid out on the page as verse. Wordsworth's meditative verse seeks both to convey a sense of thought-process in action and to engage the reader in that process. Repetition, recapitulation, sub-division, and modification, all combine in poetry which, as Herbert Lindenberger puts it, 'is not argumentative, at least not in the Augustan manner; rather it is ruminative and discursive, concerned with the wide expanse of thought existing between the extreme positions which argumentative verse normally assumes' (*On Wordsworth's 'Prelude'*, p. 65).

Such counsel is not meant to imply that the reflective passages of *The Prelude* are empty of real thought or that they are bogus, just an effect. On the contrary, no part of the poem is free of Wordsworth's intense and severe attempt to analyse, order, and make sense of his own experience. It is meant, however, to reassure the reader new to *The Prelude* that what is generally referred to as Wordsworth's 'philosophical poetry' is poetry, and not philosophy in verse. And it works, as poetry must, through rhythm, sound and image, through repetition and formal stylisation, through indirection and obliquity. Frightening though some of the meditative passages are, you do not need to have taken a course in logic, nor in European philosophy, to read them.

Chapter 3

God and Nature

Introduction

Who, or what, is the 'Wisdom and spirit of the universe' addressed in the lines quoted towards the end of the last chapter? The question cannot be avoided. Similar addresses to, or invocations of, a Spirit or a Power occur frequently throughout *The Prelude*. But nor can it be answered at all easily and even before it is approached directly some preliminary observations need to be made.

Wordsworth is clearly a profoundly religious poet. He constantly evokes experiences which have to be called spiritual or numinous, moments when the self is lost in a greater whole, when the mundane drops away and with heightened awareness 'We see into the life of things' (*Tintern Abbey*, 1. 50). The poetry celebrates mysteries. Not the mysteries of faith as such, but the mystery of man's place in the world and the wonder of the universe itself. Such celebration is one of the characteristics of the Romantic movement. However much they differed in articles of belief, Romantic poets and painters all projected a vision of what the French artist Millet called the 'infinite splendours' of human life in this world (letter, 30 May 1863).

The phrase 'religious poet' conjures up Herbert, or Milton, or Hopkins. Their work, however, brings out clearly what Wordsworth's is not. *The Temple, Paradise Lost, The Wreck of the 'Deutschland'*, all make use explicitly of elements of Christian doctrine – The Incarnation, Redemption, The Real Presence, The Second Coming. The poems cannot be understood, even at the simplest level, without knowledge of what these doctrines are. Wordsworth's poetry is not like this at all. It eschews doctrine and dogma and is not Christ-

centred. Only in 1845 did Wordsworth introduce the figure of
the Redeemer into some key passages. Before that very late
revision, all of the richest poetry was religious without being
doctrinally explicit.

To many contemporaries such a lack of specificity was
welcome. It made the poetry acceptable to people across the
sectarian divides, which widened markedly in the early nineteenth century. *Tintern Abbey* could be quoted as appositely
from an Evangelical pulpit as from an Anglo-Catholic. To
other contemporaries, however, most notably the doctrinally
suspicious dissenters, Wordsworth's lack of specificity caused
alarm. Was this evidently 'spiritual' poet a Christian or not?
That was the question asked of *The Excursion* in 1814. Wordsworth's close friend, Henry Crabb Robinson, would have liked
a clear answer, too, but despite constant probing he never
received one. In 1836 he noted in his diary that 'Wordsworth's
religion . . . would not satisfy either a religionist or a sceptic'
(*Henry Crabb Robinson on Books and Their Writers*, ed. Edith
J. Morley, 3 vols. 1938, II, p. 481).

This quotation introduces by implication an important
term, 'orthodoxy'. Critics often write about 'orthodox Christianity' and note Wordsworth's move towards it (generally
taken as signalling the decline of his powers). This language
is extremely unhelpful. There is no such thing as orthodox
Christianity. There have always been historically varying
standards of orthodoxy, upheld by the dominant power of
Church and State, against which heretics could be judged
(and in earlier times imprisoned, banished, or burnt). In
Wordsworth's time, of course, orthodoxy in England was
codified in the Thirty-Nine Articles of the Church of
England, but in reality in the eighteenth and early nineteenth
centuries everything was in dispute, not only standards of
orthodoxy but even the possibility of belief itself. Nothing is
to be gained by using a notion of orthodoxy as a starting
point for an examination of Wordsworth's beliefs.

What can be said with confidence is that in his middle years
Wordsworth began to feel more positive about the Established Church. In his youth he had been, like radicals of all

political persuasions, vehemently anti-clerical. The Established Church seemed no more than an arm of the State, its servants not ministers of the Spirit but agents of temporal power. Eventually, however, Wordsworth came to value the Anglican Church as a force for permanence and social cohesion. His life-long affection for the village church as a focus for a community, as its gathering place and the embodiment of its history, extended to include the Church as an institution, both temporal and spiritual. By 1829 he was as fierce a partisan against Catholic Emancipation as any Anglican bishop could have wished for. Whatever his private beliefs — and, as we have seen, Crabb Robinson had his doubts well after 1829 — Wordsworth was committed to the Anglican Church.

What can also be said with confidence is that all of Wordsworth's greatest poetry pre-dates the period and development just outlined. If there is a relation between Wordsworth's evolving faith and the decline of his poetic powers, it is unclear, although critics regularly pronounce on it with some certainty. Fortunately the issue is outside the concerns of this book and so no further allusion to Wordsworth's developing beliefs and religious practice after 1805 will be made.

One last point by way of preamble. An introduction to any subject ought ideally to give a bold outline, which should not be substantially modified by any complexities or loose-ends that might have to be acknowledged. Any attempt to codify or systematise Wordsworth's religious beliefs, however, runs exactly counter to what the poetry is and does. For what the abundance of the documentary evidence suggests, the fragmentary drafts perhaps even more clearly than the finished poems, is that Wordsworth was constantly exploring ideas, even as he sought to convey through the means of poetry the excitement and the passion of religious feeling. In other words, Wordsworth's ideas did not remain static and it is lost labour to assemble all the key passages in the hope that synthesised they will provide anything approaching a schedule of articles of faith.

Such a hesitant preamble might suggest that an introductory account of religious aspects of *The Prelude* could not possibly serve any useful purpose. It is not so. Varying and unsettled though they were, Wordsworth's ideas arose from, and contributed to, a particular moment of intellectual ferment which is far from the theological controversies of our own time. An introduction to that moment, and to Wordsworth's place in it, can assist reading parts of the poem which are more difficult because more historically distant.

God and Nature

Scepticism, even atheism, was not uncommon amongst the political radicals with whom Wordsworth associated in the 1790s. He knew William Godwin, the philosopher, and John Thelwall, the orator, both notorious atheists, and he certainly read the polemics of the most famous atheist of the day, Thomas Paine. But there is no evidence at all, his anti-clericalism notwithstanding, that Wordsworth was ever affected by this extreme aspect of radicalism. After first meeting him, it is true, Coleridge confided to Thelwall that he judged Wordsworth to be 'at least a *Semi*-atheist' (letter, 13 May 1796), but Coleridge was so obsessed with religion, his standard of judgement so high, that this remark cannot be taken as trustworthy evidence that Wordsworth was doubting the existence of God. The testimony of Wordsworth's poetry and letters of the period denies the possibility. And though he was chary of invoking the Deity and cautious about attributing characteristics to Him, he does in *The Prelude* give a clear definition of what he meant by God, when he refers to

> the one
> Surpassing life, which − out of space and time,
> Nor touched by welterings of passion − is,
> And hath the name of, God.

$$\text{(VI, 154--7)}$$

If the existence of God was not a live issue for Wordsworth, the question 'How can we know God?' certainly was. It is a question which arises in various ways throughout the eighteenth century in all kinds of discourse — in academic philosophy and theology, in popular Christian apologetics, in books on chemistry and physics, and in poetry. Of course the question was not a new one, but for various reasons it assumed new urgency in the later seventeenth and eighteenth centuries. Answers proposed were many and various, but two broad categories of answer dominate.

The first emphasises personal conviction. We know God because He has spoken to us as unignorably as he did to Saul. Saul's conversion and rebirth (as Paul, St Paul) is the archetype of the thousands of conversions narrated at Methodist meetings throughout the later eighteenth century. An individual bears witness that he or she has personally felt the touch of God, who is ever active in His world seeking the lost. Such personal conviction needs to be consolidated by reading the Bible, by prayer, and by good works, but without it all of these are nugatory.

The other category of answer, by contrast, stresses the operation of reason. We arrive at a conviction of God's existence through inference from evidence. The primary evidence is the world itself. In a famous illustration William Paley argued that the world was analogous to a watch. Examination of the intricate mechanisms of a watch would lead to two conclusions (1) that all its parts worked together according to a plan and (2) that there must have been an artificer. So it is with the world: God is the designer-artificer. The argument is usually known as the 'Argument from Design'. (Paley's enormously influential book, *Natural Theology; or, Evidences of the Existence and Attributes of the Deity, Collected from the Appearances of Nature*, was published in 1802, but it represented arguments he had advanced in teaching at Cambridge 1768–76 and had foreshadowed in his *Evidences of Christianity*, 1794. Versions of the 'Argument from Design' had been current, in fact, since the late seventeenth century.)

There are objections to both of these lines of argument. Personal conviction is associated with zealots, abundant in

Great Britain and America since the end of the seventeenth century, who have claimed that a personal contact with the Deity authorises them to found their own Church. Impatient of tradition or theological learning and contemptuous of ecclesiastical authority, they raise a sect simply on the basis of their assurance that they have privileged access both to God and to the meaning of Scripture. Their fervour was generally dubbed 'enthusiasm', which meant in the eighteenth century a state almost indistinguishable from madness.

To the 'Argument from Design' there are at least three main objections. First, it is so cerebral. Surely no one was ever moved to a lively sense of God through mulling over *evidence*. Second, the 'Argument from Design', which rests upon inferences and proofs with no place for imagination or leaps of faith, is too susceptible to counter arguments of a similar kind. Third, and most important, the 'Argument from Design' seems to postulate a God whose work is over. The evidences from Nature might prove the existence of a Supreme First Cause, but do they demonstrate continuing activity by the Creator or any concern for the creatures of His creation?

In Wordsworth's poetry aspects of both of these traditions of religious thought fuse. The religious affirmation is grounded on an intellectual base, but it is made, joyously, as an affirmation because of the intensity of the poet's experience and conviction.

The 'Argument from Design' is not stated in the poetry, but it is implicit in Wordsworth's reverent response to the natural world. When he was seventy-three years old, Wordsworth recalled *the* formative moment in his poetic life. It was not the discovery of a great model, of Milton or Shakespeare, nor the publication of schoolboy verses. What Wordsworth remembered was once noticing the outline of an oak against the sun setting in the west. From that moment, he said, 'I date . . . my consciousness of the infinite variety of natural appearances' (note to *An Evening Walk*). His passion for seeing, he declares, determined the nature of his poetic career. Quotation is hardly necessary to support the point. The evidence is overwhelming. *A Night-Piece*, for example, describes a natural phenomenon, with attention both to detail and the overall effect of the scene, as if rendering homage to the world is a self-evidently valuable act. One of Wordsworth's fellow-students at Cambridge recalled him 'speaking very highly in praise of the beauties of the North; with a warmth indeed which, at that time, appeared to me hardly short of enthusiasm' (Gill, *William Wordsworth: A Life*, p. 43). Clearly Paley was not needed. Wordsworth already knew how much the natural world offered as a subject for contemplation and as a source of delight.

Wordsworth's greatest poetry takes us far beyond Paley's methodical demonstration that the evidence of Nature proves the existence of a Creator. In passage after passage, especially in the years 1797–1800, Wordsworth explores his conviction that God is ever-present in the world, literally sustaining His creation moment by moment. God is not the artificer of an intricate machine, but the inspirer of a living whole, in which animate and the supposedly inanimate course with the energy of the One Life, the power

> Of something far more deeply interfused,
> Whose dwelling is the light of setting suns,
> And the round ocean, and the living air,
> And the blue sky, and in the mind of man,
> A motion and a spirit, that impels
> All thinking things, all objects of all thought,
> And rolls through all things.
>
> (*Tintern Abbey*, 97–103)

There is no doubt that Wordsworth's formulations were strongly influenced by Coleridge, in his own words 'a Library-Cormorant', whose unceasing search for an intellectual point of rest drove him through most important British and European philosophers and theologians, and through many who are no more than footnotes to intellectual history. 'We see our God everywhere – the Universe in the most literal Sense is his written Language', he wrote in 1795 (*Lectures 1795 On Politics and Religion*, p. 339), and explored this affirmation in his 'Conversation Poems', *The Eolian Harp,*

This Lime-Tree Bower my Prison, and *Frost at Midnight*, and in his now little read, but very important, *Religious Musings*. (For an introduction to Coleridge's thought on religion, see H. W. Piper, *The Active Universe*; Thomas McFarland, *Coleridge and the Pantheist Tradition* (Oxford, 1969); Owen Barfield, *What Coleridge Thought* (Middletown, Conn., 1971); and for his influence on Wordsworth's thinking, Jonathan Wordsworth, *The Music of Humanity*.)

Even at their moment of greatest intimacy, however, when Wordsworth was drinking deep Coleridgean draughts, a crucial difference between the two poets was emerging. Put simply it is that Coleridge saw philosophical problems and was goaded by them to further study and refinement of thought. Wordsworth, on the other hand saw philosophical problems, but was not tormented by them. He explored, whereas Coleridge wanted to get things straight. Keats put it brilliantly when he said that Coleridge was 'incapable of re-maining content with half knowledge' (letter, 21 December 1817). Wordsworth was.

It is important that this point is not misunderstood. The argument is not that Wordsworth was a shoddy or lazy philosopher, but rather that he put the interests of poetry before those of philosophy. To give one example. In a 1798 fragment (printed in 'The Norton *Prelude*', p. 496), Words-worth tries to define his sense of 'that one interior life',

> In which all beings live with God, themselves
> Are God, existing in one mighty whole,
> As undistinguishable as the cloudless east
> At noon is from the cloudless west, when all
> The hemisphere is one cerulean blue.

The theological implications of this image are giddying. They certainly troubled Coleridge, who was already in 1796 agonis-ing over whether such a pantheist position was strictly distinguishable from atheism (see letter, 20 March 1796). Or another example. In *The Prelude*, II, 395–434 (dealt with in more detail in the next chapter), Wordsworth allows the possibility that his perception of the One Life was not direct access to 'the power of truth / Coming in revelation', but the result of his own transference of enjoyment on to 'unorganic natures', thus 'Coercing all things into sympathy'.

Both of these passages raise important questions, and there is no reason to doubt that Wordsworth appreciated their significance, but no attempt is made in later poetry to *settle* them. For Coleridge this degree of uncertainty about topics as important as pantheism, or the relation of inner and outer, self and the not-self, was eventually intolerable. His later prose, of which *Biographia Literaria* is only the best-known work, represents a sustained and rigorous intellectual effort at clarification of such crucial problems. Far from finding uncertainty poetically crippling, however, Wordsworth seems to have been able to build on it.

Transition lines immediately following the passage last mentioned suggest why:

> If this be error, and another faith
> Find easier access to the pious mind,
> Yet were I grossly destitute of all
> Those human sentiments which make this earth
> So dear if I should fail with grateful voice
> To speak of you, ye mountains, and ye lakes
> And sounding cataracts, ye mists and winds
> That dwell among the hills where I was born.
>
> (II, 435–42)

Wordsworth concedes that others might find his account of the One Life inadequate, perhaps unacceptable, as a philosophical-theological formulation, and the concession is made ungrudgingly because he is not interested in pursuing philosophical implications nor in persuading through proofs. What Wordsworth is doing is bearing witness to an all-consuming personal experience:

> I was only then
> Contented when with bliss ineffable
> I felt the sentiment of being spread
> O'er all that moves, and all that seemeth still,
> O'er all that, lost beyond the reach of thought
> And human knowledge, to the human eye
> Invisible, yet liveth to the heart,
>
> . . .

> in all things
> I saw one life, and felt that it was joy.

(II, 418–30)

This poetry offers not *proof*, but testimony of *conviction*.

It was this Wordsworth who spoke to many throughout the nineteenth century. Profoundly religious people such as Carlyle, Ruskin, Tennyson, to mention only famous names, who could no longer believe in, or feel anything for, the official formulations of Anglican doctrine, found in his poetry a religious testimony to which they could respond. William Hale White, who wrote as 'Mark Rutherford', testified that it was as rain to his spirit parched by seasons of arid dissenting doctrine: 'Instead of an object of worship which was altogether artificial, remote, never coming into genuine contact with me, I had now one which I thought to be real, one in which literally I could live and move and have my being . . . Wordsworth did for me what every religious reformer has done, – he re-created my Supreme Divinity' (*The Autobiography of Mark Rutherford*, edited by His Friend Reuben Shapcott, 1881, 2nd revised edn 1912, p. 19).

Moral implications

If God exists and the world is 'in the most literal Sense his written Language', what are the moral implications of this fact for human beings?

In Christian doctrine the answer is that the question has been settled through Revelation. Through Christ God intervened in the world, identifying Himself in personal form, and making known to man the providential design for his destiny. Through Holy Scripture, God's law, whose writ runs through every aspect of life, has likewise been revealed.

The emphasis in Wordsworth's poetry is quite different. In both simple lyrics and complex blank verse alike, Wordsworth declares that direct communion with the Godhead in Nature, the reading of his 'written Language', has a moral effect in itself. Wordsworth does not scorn the Bible record, nor attack in any form the Trinitarian faith in the divinity of

Christ. These key elements in Christian Revelation are simply disregarded. In their place are repeated explorations of a conviction that intense communion with the grand and permanent forms of Nature moulds the human being to beneficial ends.

At a simple level this is easily appreciated. In 1798 Coleridge explained to his brother that he had snapped his 'squeaking baby-trumpet of Sedition' and had retired to the country. After years of being agitated by the events of immediate political life, he was now musing on 'fundamental & general causes'. He loved 'fields & woods & mountains with almost a visionary fondness' and was discovering that 'benevolence & quietness' were growing within him 'as that fondness . . . increased' (10 March 1798). Twentieth-century readers, heirs to the Romantic view of Nature, with access to National Parks which are one of its legacies, will have no difficulty in following what Coleridge clearly felt he had to spell out. And, of course, the idea survives, in a vague, semi-religious form, that climbing mountains, being quiet, and absorbing the beauty of a landscape, does one good.

But there is nothing of this wishy-washy vagueness about Wordsworth's position. In 1798 he explicated his beliefs at length, and with great care, in a passage which begins:

> Not useless do I deem
> These quiet sympathies with things that hold
> An inarticulate language, for the man
> Once taught to love such objects as excite
> No morbid passions, no disquietude,
> No vengeance and no hatred, needs must feel
> The joy of that pure principle of love
> So deeply that, unsatisfied with aught
> Less pure and exquisite, he cannot choose
> But seek for objects of a kindred love
> In fellow-natures, and a kindred joy.
>
> (1–11)

The passage, originally intended as a possible conclusion to *The Ruined Cottage* is far too long to quote here. It is printed in the *Oxford Authors: Wordsworth*, pp. 678–80, together with a complementary meditation on the 'active principle alive in all things'.

'Not useless do I deem' is situated squarely in the line of eighteenth-century associationist psychology, which ultimately derives from the philosophy of John Locke, in which the fully-formed mind is conceived of as a product of the stimuli which have acted on it from the moment of the baby's first exposure to the phenomenal world. (Chapter 8 of Basil Willey's *The Eighteenth-Century Background* remains the best introduction to this subject.) Through exposure to the beneficial influence of 'such objects as excite / No morbid passions, no disquietude', the human being, the passage argues, will learn to love and seek for objects of love. Eventually one passes from love of Nature to love of Man and,

> Thus disciplined
> All things shall live in us, and we shall live
> In all things that surround us. This I deem
> Our tendency, and thus shall every day
> Enlarge our sphere of pleasure and of pain.
> For thus the senses and the intellect
> Shall each to each supply a mutual aid,
> Invigorate and sharpen and refine
> Each other with a power that knows no bound,
> And forms and feelings acting thus, and thus
> Reacting, they shall acquire
> A living spirit and a character
> Till then unfelt, and each be multiplied,
> With a variety that knows no end.
> Thus deeply drinking in the soul of things
> We shall be wise perforce, and we shall move
> From strict necessity along the path
> Of order and of good.

(78–95)

The whole argument is so tightly presented, in a series of propositions which build to the conclusion, that selective quotation is more than usually brutal and unhelpful. These excerpts, however, suggest the importance of 'Not useless do I deem' and its centrality to Wordsworth's poetry. It is directly linked to every passage in *The Prelude* in which the growth of the poet's mind is related to communion with Nature. It helps one understand the astonishing declaration in *Tintern Abbey* that the poet is

> well pleased to recognize
> In nature and the language of the sense,
> The anchor of my purest thoughts, the nurse,
> The guide, the guardian of my heart, and soul
> Of all my moral being.
>
> (108–112)

It underpins Wordsworth's repeated assertion, adumbrated most fully in Book VIII of *The Prelude*, that love of Nature leads to love of Man. And it is the metaphysical foundation of such lyrics as *Lines Written in Early Spring* and 'It is the first mild day of March'.

Two further points need to be made. The first is that 'Not useless do I deem' is not a 'key' to the Wordsworthian code. As has already been stressed, Wordsworth's poetry is exploratory. The passage propounds ideas which are the basis of Wordsworth's work during his most innovative period, but it is not an all-inclusive *credo*. Over the years to come Wordsworth refined and developed ideas, most notably on the place of Imagination in moral growth, and many drafts of blank verse disclose attempts to explore further some of the implications of the main argument of 'Not useless do I deem'.

The second point that the passage only matters because it is here that Wordsworth most clearly explicates the psychological, theological, and philosophical ground work of his convictions. It is a passage to which one can point to counter the accusation that Wordsworth's beliefs are nebulous. But it is not itself great poetry, nor is it at the heart of Wordsworth's achievement as a poet. For it is imaginatively inert and all of Wordsworth's powers are bent in his finest work to arousal, to the awakening of passion, to the penetration of what he once called 'the blood & vital juices of our minds'. Conviction of what it means to participate in the One Life must seize the reader, who, as Wordsworth said in a note to *The Thorn*, 'cannot be too often reminded that Poetry is passion'. This is the work of the lyrics, the great narratives, *The Ruined Cottage* and *Michael*, and above all of *The Prelude*.

Chapter 4

The Poem

'Motions retrograde': introduction

I said unto the life which I had lived,
'Where art thou? Hear I not a voice from thee
Which 'tis reproach to hear?' Anon I rose
As if on wings, and saw beneath me stretched
Vast prospect of the world which I had been,
And was; and hence this song . . .

In these lines (XIII, 375–80), almost at the end of *The Prelude*, Wordsworth gives an account both of its genesis and its manner of proceeding. Like a hovering bird, the poet surveys the vast world that is his own being. He can at will move across its extent in space and time. But he is also interrogating his life, asking 'Where art thou?', and in the answers he hears reproach. Framing the right questions is itself an act of interpretation. Understanding the answers is another.

Not surprisingly, a poem which is both an exercise in mapping and an interrogation is a difficult one to grasp. It opens with a rapturous welcome to freedom and inspiration at the present moment, 'Oh there is blessing in this gentle breeze, / That blows from the green fields . . .', so it comes as a shock to discover at line 55 that this effusion is not a spontaneous utterance introducing this poem, *now*, but the recollection of an outpouring in the past, which led nowhere: 'the harp / Was soon defrauded, and the banded host / Of harmony dispersed in straggling sounds, / And lastly utter silence' (I, 104–7). The poem closes with warm memories of the Alfoxden summer of 1798, when *Lyrical Ballads* was shaped and *The Recluse* conceived. This recollection, however, acts not as a graceful closure to a chronological sequence which has now reached its natural end, but as the preamble to a final twenty-five-line dedication to holy labour, a work of redemption 'surely yet to come' (XIII, 441)

The Prelude thus opens with a sense of great tasks to be accomplished and it closes with the same sense. It concludes as it began, as a threshold to *The Recluse*. But although the structure overall, seen from this distant view, is non-linear, much of the body of the poem is sufficiently chronological to give the impression that it is following the development of a life in time. The problem is, however, that Wordsworth plays fast and loose with chronology in a variety of ways, whose ultimate effect is to dissolve confidence in chronology as a structuring principle at all. Years are sometimes elided – the whole of Wordsworth's early childhood, for example, in five lines (I, 305–9) – or just glanced at – term-time at Cambridge, for example. Formative experiences are highlighted, but their temporal relationship is obscured. Thus Wordsworth's crossing of the Alps, which occurred in 1790, is placed historically in the text by dateable references to Revolutionary France, but the ascent of Snowdon, which was made a year later, is not. In fact, if one followed up the chronological pointer at the opening to Book XIII, 'In one of these excursions', one would have to conclude that Wordsworth climbed Snowdon after his sojourn in France and after his solitary ordeal on Salisbury Plain, that is, in 1793. The historical chronicle 1793–5 is dense with dateable allusions to the outbreak of war, the rise and fall of Robespierre, the change of direction in French military strategy and so on, unlike the account of Wordsworth's crisis and recovery 1794–7, which is barren of chronological markers which might enable the reader to assess how long the crisis lasted or in what way his recovery was, or was not, related to contemporary political events.

One's sense of the fluidity of chronology in this poem is also heightened by those moments when the poet steps out of one chronological flow – that is, the history of his own life 1770–98 – to draw attention to another, the temporal dimension of the poem's composition. Book II, for example, leads in conclusion directly from an account of Wordsworth's seventeenth year to a personal statement about 'these times of fear' (II, 448), that is, the late 1790s. Book VII opens by revealing that the introductory lines of the poem were composed five years ago and that the poet has recently been having difficulty making progress, before suddenly plunging back into the historical chronicle with, 'Returned from that excursion, soon I bade farewell' (VII, 57–8). Book IX similarly opens with a confession, in the present tense, that the poem has for a long time been making 'motions retrograde' (18), before historical reporting reasserts itself with 'Free as a colt at pasture on the hills / I ranged at large through the metropolis / Month after month' (IX, 18–20).

Clearly Wordsworth's disregard of chronology, and his repeated reminders that this is a poem which it is taking many years to write, serve his purpose of analysing, not just recording experience. *The Prelude* is organised, in other words, not chronologically but thematically. The summary by M. H. Abrams in *Natural Supernaturalism* (required reading for any student of Romanticism) cannot be bettered: '*The Prelude* . . . is ordered in three stages. There is a process of mental development which, although at times suspended, remains a continuum; this process is violently broken by a crisis of apathy and despair; but the mind then recovers an integrity which, despite admitted losses, is represented as a level higher than the initial unity, in that the mature mind possesses powers, together with an added range, depth, and sensitivity of awareness, which are the products of the critical experiences it has undergone' (p. 77).

Such an assured account of the poem's structure, however, (and this is not a critical judgement on M. H. Abrams) will not prepare anyone new to the poem for what the actual experience of reading it is like. Far from breathing assurance, *The Prelude* proceeds through a sequence of explorations and tentative statements, in which recapitulations and modifications suggest a dynamic and unending process of discovery. Repeatedly the poet declares what his theme is, and towards the end of the poem these declarations become more frequent and insistent, as if he were determined to impose a highly

visible thematic order on his own creation. But the poem
resists it. The reader will find obscurities and difficulties that
remain difficult and obscure on repeated readings, sub-texts
that provoke questions that threaten to subvert the surface
coherence. *The Prelude* is not a monologic, unruffled poem.
As Kenneth Johnston has acutely remarked, 'the sensation of
losing one's way that occurs in reading almost every book of
The Prelude . . . properly accompanies every re-reading of the
poem' (*Wordsworth and 'The Recluse'*, p. 122). Johnston is
right and it is not part of the purpose of this chapter to provide a map which makes it impossible for the reader to go
astray. What is offered instead is a discussion of the main
movements of *The Prelude*, a foregrounding of its most
significant elements, which, if it helps the reader feel his / her
way into the poem, will properly make itself eventually
redundant.

'Heroic argument': the opening

Where does *The Prelude* begin? An odd question, but it is an
odd beginning. The poem actually opens with the effusion
mentioned above, in which the poet exults in a sense of
freedom which finds confirmation in the breeze, the clouds,
a running stream. The wind that beats against his cheek is
matched by a 'corresponding mild creative breeze' (43)
within, which soon becomes a storm, breaking up the frost
with vernal intimations. This welcome to power, however,
which would make a strong opening to a poem, turns out to
be no such thing, for though the joy and freedom led to a contented settlement in life, 'complete / Composure, and the
happiness entire' (121–2), they did not bear fruit in writing.
Oppressed by 'phantoms of conceit / That had been floating
loose about so long' (130–1), the poet braces himself to a
definite work – but what work?

Wordsworth has presented a comparable moment in which
a note of strenuous endeavour is checked by incertitude in
Home at Grasmere, written largely in 1800. In this poem,
conceived of as the first book of *The Recluse*, the poet

celebrates his joy at finding his true abiding place. Recognising the privilege which Providence has bestowed, however, also entails acknowledgement of the burden of duty:

> But 'tis not to enjoy, for this alone
> That we exist; no, something must be done.
>
> (875–6)

But here, too, the poet feels the urgency of his duty more strongly than any commitment to a particular task which he could fulfill *as a writer*. *Home at Grasmere* ends with a magnificent statement of what the poet's life-work must be, but not with any clear specification of what form in poetry the work might take.

At the opening of *The Prelude* Wordsworth engages more directly with this issue. Whereas Milton announces his theme in six lines of *Paradise Lost*, but confesses his human inadequacy to such a great enterprise ('And chiefly thou O Spirit . . . what in me is dark / Illumine, what is low raise and support'), Wordsworth begins his poem by declaring himself strong in all necessary poetic powers, but unsure of a subject. In lines 177–228, topic after topic is paraded as a possibility – a British romance, a story from Norse myth or the classics, perhaps an exemplary tale of human fortitude from European history, or perhaps a narrative of the poet's own invention on a topic 'more near akin / To my own passions and habitual thoughts' (221–2). Finally the poet confesses that his 'last and favorite aspiration' is that he should write

> some philosophic song
> Of truth that cherishes our daily life,
> With meditations passionate from deep
> Recesses in man's heart.
>
> (230–3)

But he also confesses that from the burden of such a task he takes refuge in procrastination and in the thought that he is not yet mature enough to succeed. Ambition is checked by fear, courage by humility, so paralysingly that the poet images himself as

> Unprofitably travelling towards the grave,
> Like a false steward who hath much received
> And renders nothing back.

(269–71)

And only then, with the question 'Was it for this . . .', which is also a self-admonition and self-reproach, does Wordsworth begin the narrative of his life.

This is an astonishingly hesitant opening to a poem of epic scale, but what must be recognised is that this hesitancy is a literary strategy. When Wordsworth wrote the opening 271 lines of *The Prelude* he had already composed the greater part of the whole poem. He knew his subject and had confidence in his powers. Yet the introduction to the poem suggests uncertainty about both.

The effect of this literary strategy is threefold. First, it directs attention to the poet as himself, not as a voice of the Muses or as an instrument of the Holy Spirit, or as a timeless minstrel or bard, but as a self-dependent, creative being, awed by the possession of special powers, yet fearful of the responsibilities they entail. This is to be a poem about being, or becoming, a poet and compared with that theme historical romance or fictional narratives become secondary:

> O heavens, how awful is the might of souls,
> And what they do within themselves
>   . . .
> This is in truth heroic argument.

(III, 178–82)

Second, the opening suggests that this is to be a poem of exploration and discovery. The question, 'Was it for this', has to be answered. But, the introduction implies, the poet as yet has no answer. What might be said will only be discovered through reflection upon and analysis of experience and *through writing it down*. The answer to the question is to be nothing less than the poem itself, but what that poem will be remains, after 271 lines of introduction, unclear.

Finally, it conveys the sense that the poem is to be a test of the poet's worthiness for another and greater task. The 'holy life of music and of verse' (54) must be dedicated to the 'philosophic song / Of truth' (230–1), but to that great work the poet declares himself unequal. *The Prelude* therefore presents itself as a trial. Insofar as the poet identifies his theme and embodies it in powerful verse, the poem will affirm its creator's adequacy for the greater task which alone justifies this autobiographical prelude. Each moment when the poet inspects the progress of his own work (as distinct from his own life's progress, which has been anterior to the poem) confirms the sense that the poem is a test of his power. The magnificent concluding lines of *The Prelude* are a declaration that the poet has come through.

'Fair seed-time': childhood and youth

After a day of boisterous exertion Wordsworth and his friends row across Windermere, homewards towards the western shore and Hawkshead:

> But ere the fall
> Of night, when in our pinnace we returned
> Over the dusky lake, and to the beach
> Of some small island steered our course, with one,
> The minstrel of our troop, and left him there,
> And rowed off gently, while he blew his flute
> Alone upon the rock, oh, then the calm
> And dead still water lay upon my mind
> Even with a weight of pleasure, and the sky,
> Never before so beautiful, sank down
> Into my heart and held me like a dream.
>
> (II, 170–80)

This beautiful passage is characteristic of many such in the first two books of *The Prelude*, which celebrate the intense experiences of childhood with a power unparalleled in English poetry. The 'common range of visible things' (II, 182) is transformed by natural means, by twilight, by reflection from the surface of the water, by stillness, and is so deeply internalised by the boy as pleasure, that the external and the internal fuse. The sky sinks *down into* the boy's heart and holds him with the power of dream.

Elsewhere the penetration of the child's whole being

follows physical exertion, as in the 'Skating' episode (I, 452–89), the 'Birds'-Nesting' (I, 333–50), or 'The Robbing of the Snares' (I, 310–32), and in perhaps the most important episode of all, 'The Stolen Boat' (I, 372–426), it is the product of fear. In this incident, which takes place at night, the boy unties a boat on the shore of Ullswater and rows proudly out towards the middle of the lake. He fixes his gaze upon a peak which is the bound of the horizon, but as he rows away from the shore his angle of vision relative to the peak changes, with the result that another, previously hidden peak, comes into view and looms larger with every stroke of the oars. His heart beating with guilt at 'stealing' the boat, the boy rows ever more strongly to evade the sight, but the huge cliff strides out across the lake in pursuit of the miscreant and he only escapes by rowing back to shore. But though he creeps away safe, the conquest of his mind continues:

> and after I had seen
> That spectacle, for many days my brain
> Worked with a dim and undetermined sense
> Of unknown modes of being. In my thoughts
> There was a darkness — call it solitude
> Or blank desertion — no familiar shapes
> Of hourly objects, images of trees,
> Of sea or sky, no colours of green fields,
> But huge and mighty forms that do not live
> Like living men moved slowly through my mind
> By day, and were the trouble of my dreams.
>
> (I, 417–26)

In some experiences the boy's senses are heightened to an extraordinary awareness of natural phenomena — 'With what strange utterance did the loud dry wind / Blow through my ears' (I, 348–9). In others there is no Impressionist sharpening, rather a melting fusion of mind, senses, and Nature. Common to all is the intensest possible sensation of being alive.

The climax of these books at II, 405–34 is a hymn to what D. H. Lawrence, the last of the great Romantics, was to call in his *Apocalypse* the 'rapture' of being alive and 'part of the living, incarnate cosmos':

                    I was only then
Contented when with bliss ineffable
I felt the sentiment of being spread
O'er all that moves, and all that seemeth still,
O'er all that, lost beyond the reach of thought
And human knowledge, to the human eye
Invisible, yet liveth to the heart,
O'er all that leaps, and runs, and shouts, and sings,
Or beats the gladsome air, o'er all that glides
Beneath the wave, yea, in the wave itself
And mighty depth of waters. Wonder not
If such my transports were, for in all things
I saw one life, and felt that it was joy.

This is the language both of the Psalmist and of John and
Charles Wesley, but it is important to note that it is
theologically unspecific. In the comparably exultant *Tintern
Abbey* (1798), Wordsworth hymns his communion with the
Ultimate Power through

              a sense sublime
Of something far more deeply interfused,
Whose dwelling is the light of setting suns,
And the round ocean, and the living air,
And the blue sky, and in the mind of man,
A motion and a spirit, that impels
All thinking things, all objects of all thought,
And rolls through all things.

                                              (96–103)

In both passages the poet's *jubilate* wells up not through
awareness of a personally knowable God, still less from conviction of salvation through the sacrifice of Christ, but from
a total, over-mastering absorption in the life of an *active*
universe.

Books I and II are the foundation of *The Prelude*. The
childhood experiences themselves substantiate the poet's
claim that his soul had 'Fair seed-time' (I, 305). That they retain their hold on his memory and empower poetry of such
beauty validates all that the poem says later about memory's
redemptive function. But they are also the foundation of the
poem philosophically. The word is not helpful. *The Prelude*
is not a philosophical treatise. 'Argument', however, won't

really do either, since in modern usage it suggests that the poem is a construction of points designed to end in a specific conclusion, and it is not. But some such word as 'philosophically' is needed, for *The Prelude* is a poem in which thought is brought to bear upon experience, and its ground is established in these opening books.

Wordsworth makes a number of propositions which are to be explored, modified, and ultimately validated in the rest of the poem. The first is that he was a 'chosen son' (III, 82). The religious associations of the phrase are not accidental. Looking back over his life the poet acknowledges, not that he was unique, or that the context of his early life was the only possible one in which a human being could develop – both would be absurd claims – but that for him it seems as if the nurturing power of the 'Wisdom and spirit of the universe' (I, 427) had exercised parental care, ensuring that ultimately he should become a 'Prophet of Nature' (XIII, 442), and a great poet.

The second is that coming to consciousness, engaging from infancy with the phenomenal world, is itself an imaginative act. In an astonishing passage on infant psychology (II, 237–80) Wordsworth emphasises the *activity* of the child's mind as it establishes its sense of self in the world:

> Emphatically such a being lives,
> An inmate of this active universe.
>   . . .
>   his mind,
> Even as an agent of the one great mind,
> Creates, creator and receiver both,
> Working but in alliance with the works
> Which it beholds.

This is 'the first / Poetic spirit of our human life' (II, 275–6), our 'first creative sensibility' (II, 379). In this sense, all men are potentially poets, imaginative, creative beings. The general human tragedy is that in most people imagination is 'By uniform controul of after years . . . abated and suppressed' (II, 277–8). In the artist it may remain 'Preeminent till death' (II, 280).

The third proposition is that all that is strongest and best in the poet's being grows from these formative years. Switching to the present (1799) at the end of Book II, Wordsworth confidently declares:

>   if, in this time
> Of dereliction and dismay, I yet
> Despair not of our nature, but retain
> A more than Roman confidence, a faith
> That fails not, in all sorrow my support,
> The blessing of my life, the gift is yours
> Ye mountains, thine, O Nature. Thou hast fed
> My lofty speculations, and in thee
> For this uneasy heart of ours I find
> A never-failing principle of joy
> And purest passion.
>
> (II, 456–66)

Wordsworth was writing at a dark time. Government Bills introduced in 1795, which were intended to suppress political activity and to stifle the expression of anti-government opinion, had proved very effective. A network of spies and informers suborned and eroded popular dissent. Even so courageous a figure as John Thelwall had been silenced by hired bullies, who broke up his lectures and hounded him from town to town (see Nicholas Roe, *Wordsworth and Coleridge: The Radical Years* and Albert Goodwin, *The Friends of Liberty*). Others who had once supported the French cause loudly proclaimed their conversion, as Napoleon prosecuted ever more ruthlessly a war of aggression against the whole of Europe. But Wordsworth declares he retains 'A more than Roman confidence'. He lives, that is, not only like Seneca, who maintained individual dignity and rationality even in Nero's Rome, but confident, as Seneca could not be, that eventually the best in 'our nature' would triumph.

The rest of the poem is to explore the meaning of this 'dereliction and dismay' passage and to give an account of what has had to be undergone before its confident hope could be uttered as an article of faith.

Education: true and false

A descriptive summary account of Books III to V might read: in various ways these books concern the conflict between true and false education. The narrative of Wordsworth's early years at Cambridge depicts the sterility of institutionalised learning. Book IV shows how easily festivity and gregariousness, a necessary part of youth, can become time-wasting. In Book V the poet passionately opposes the prevailing orthodoxies of contemporary education.

Such a summary, however, though an accurate enough placing of these books in the architectonics of *The Prelude* as a whole, would be untrue to the poem if it did not concede that the conflicts presented are bogus. In real life such conflicts of course exist and it may be that at times the young Wordsworth felt their pressure in his own. But as they are presented by the mature poet the conflicts are so one-sided that there is no real struggle at all. The form of dialectical opposition between claim and counter-claim exists only to enable a massive re-affirmation of the values that were established in the opening books.

Consider, for example, the presentation of Cambridge. A narrative which deftly evokes an undergraduate's excitement at entering a new world, with its own uniform, customs, and demands, passes with what any university teacher is going to feel is unseemly haste over 'college labours . . . the lecturer's room' (III, 60), only to end abruptly at line 81 in a lengthy passage in which the poet sweeps aside all that has gone before as unimportant compared with the sustaining truth that he was a 'chosen son'. For 114 lines, some of *The Prelude*'s finest verse, Wordsworth celebrates the powers of mind he took with him to Cambridge and which he exercised against its deadening influence:

> now I felt
> The strength and consolation which were mine.
> As if awakened, summoned, rouzed, constrained,
> I looked for universal things, perused
> The common countenance of earth and heaven,

And, turning the mind in upon itself,
Pored, watched, expected, listened, spread my thoughts,
And spread them with a wider creeping, felt
Incumbences more awful, visitings
Of the upholder, of the tranquil soul,
Which underneath all passion lives secure
A steadfast life.

(III, 107–18)

Declaring that

Unknown, unthought of, yet I was most rich,
I had a world about me – 'twas my own,
I made it; for it only lived to me,
And to the God who looked into my mind

(III, 141–4)

Wordsworth concludes with a recapitulation of the 'one life'
passage in Book II, 405–34.

It is clear that the poet looks back on Cambridge as a threat
to his imaginative development, but from the poetry itself it
is impossible to sense that the threat was real. The passage
just quoted demonstrates that Wordsworth was already en-
dowed with what no university could bestow or take away.
The satirical sketches and the reflections that constitute the
rest of Book III establish Cambridge as a crowded tragi-
comic stage, on which the poet had only a walk-on part, but
they do not establish that Wordsworth's imaginative
autonomy was in danger.

In Book IV a key statement of personal strength similarly
arises from a context in which the poet has been stressing its
opposite. Much of this book is a touching recollection of the
undergraduate's return in his long vacation to his real home,
Hawkshead. He hails old friends with renewed delight,
quickens his steps at the sight of the village church, greets the
old lady with whom he lodged, who as his surrogate mother
sheds some tears 'While she perused me with a parent's pride'
(18), and wanders about noticing what has changed since his
departure:

Why should I speak of what a thousand hearts
Have felt, and every man alive can guess?

(33–4)

As the narrative proceeds, however, Wordsworth suggests that though he 'Loved deeply, all that I had loved before' (270), his pleasure in 'gawds / And feast and dance and public revelry / And sports and games' (273–5) puts him in danger of blotting out experience of lasting value with a 'vague heartless chace / Of trivial pleasures' (302–3). Hardly has he uttered this severe self-admonition, however, when he recalls that the most important moment of the whole vacation arose out of just such a trivial pleasure as those he has been censuring. Wordsworth has passed the night 'in dancing, gaiety and mirth', and now sets off to walk home alone:

> Magnificent
> The morning was, a memorable pomp
> More glorious than I ever had beheld.
> The sea was laughing at a distance; all
> The solid mountains were bright as clouds,
> Grain-tinctured, drenched in empyrean light;
> And in the meadows and the lower grounds
> Was all the sweetness of a common dawn –
> Dews, vapours, and the melody of birds,
> And labourers going forth into the fields.
> Ah, need I say, dear friend, that to the brim
> My heart was full? I made no vows, but vows
> Were then made for me: bond unknown to me
> Was given, that I should be – else sinning greatly –
> A dedicated spirit. On I walked
> In blessedness, which even yet remains.

> (330–45)

In that 'all the sweetness of a common dawn' Wordsworth once again identifies the terrain over which his imagination holds imperious sway. No experience yet revealed in the poem comes near to challenging its power.

In Book V the dynamics of affirmation work in a similar way, but the materials of the book are so odd, and the connections of thought so opaque, that it is not surprising that many readers find this one of the most recalcitrant books of the whole poem.

It opens with a lament, both explicit and implicit in a dream allegory, for the frailty of books, for the fact that the imperishable mind has no medium on which to stamp its impress of like permanence. Wordsworth then hymns great writers 'as powers / For ever to be hallowed' (219–20), before launching into a 200-line onslaught on modern theories of education which, stressing book-learning and the accumulation of fact, produce child-prodigies, monstrous distortions of natural growth. Against such pedagogic control Wordsworth urges freedom, the freedom of the boy who hoots to the owls across Windermere, the freedom of the imagination to lose itself in *The Arabian Nights*, the freedom to learn by indirection and delight.

Wordsworth's passion arises from experience. He had encountered at last one well-meaning zealot, Thomas Wedgwood, who believed that a rigorously controlled education could hasten the perfection of man. An account of Wedgwood's scheme can be found in my biography *William Wordsworth: A Life*, pp. 130–1. One of Wedgwood's propositions was that the child being brought up under ideal conditions 'must never go out of doors or leave his own apartment'. Wordsworth never wavered in his opposite conviction. As late as 1845 he was urging on an Inspector of Schools an enlightened approach to the education of small children, excusing his unorthodox attitudes by declaring that he spoke as one 'who spent half of his boyhood in running wild among the Mountains' (letter to Hugh Tremenheere, 16 December 1845). There are many kinds of bad education, however, and in singling out rote-learning Wordsworth is not highlighting a torture to which he has been exposed. On the contrary, all his recollections of Hawkshead Grammar School dwell on the enlightened and humane manner of instruction there. What he is doing is identifying, and magnifying for effect, the most obvious enemy to all that he valued in his own education. Book V re-affirms the primacy of Imagination, grounded in Nature, fostered and strengthened by books. And the process of growing, *The Prelude* asserts, must be in that order.

'Paramount endowment in the mind': Book VI

Book VI performs many functions. Its function in the

narrative, the forward-moving aspect of *The Prelude*, is to
expose Wordsworth to experience beyond the known and
understood world of home. In France, Switzerland, and Italy
the poet is a traveller, not a sojourner. Politics enter the
poem, obliquely, prefiguring their centrality in future narrative. Structurally, too, Book VI is highly significant. Once
one's first linear reading of *The Prelude* is completed, it
stands out that Books VI and XIII parallel each other, the
second being the richer for experiences of which the first is
innocent.

Thematically Book VI is clearly central. Its concern, expressed variously through narrative, meditations, and
apostrophe, is with the 'paramount endowment in the mind'
(153), with Imagination, both as a topic for contemplation
and as a power.

In a sense Book VI is also a paradigm for the whole poem,
in that it exhibits most fascinatingly just how complex was
Wordsworth's relation to his material. One thread of the
book is narrative of recollected experience. The poet returns
to Cambridge, leaps over two academic years, walks across
France, crosses the Alps, travels in northern Italy, and returns
for the opening of Book VII to London. As he remembers the
welcome given to the English travellers by the joyous French,
the dancing and the feasting that delayed their onward rush
towards the Alps, and as he records at a much slower pace the
ight of Mont Blanc, the crossing of the Alps, and his discomfiting adventures around Lake Como, Wordsworth goes back
to 1790, to places and experiences which nourished his
imagination for much of his adult life. Equally important,
however, is the mind's activity in the here-and-now, that is
during composition in 1804. Throughout the book the illusion
of historical time, conjured in a narrative that tries faithfully
to record the feelings of 1790, is broken by urgent imaginative
engagement with and in the present.

One example of this counterpoint is the address to Coleridge (246–60). Recalling how in vacations he rambled in
Dovedale, Yorkshire and the Border Country, Wordsworth
celebrates the joy that crowned all others, his reunion with his

sister, Dorothy (208–18). Next he draws his future wife Mary in to his memory (233–45), when suddenly desire for what was not overtakes him. Coleridge ought to have completed this group of those whom Wordsworth loved best, but they had not yet met him. Desire fulfills what memory denies:

> O friend, we had not seen thee at that time,
> And yet a power is on me and a strong
> Confusion, and I seem to plant thee there.
>
> (246–8)

So strong is the desire, in fact, that the image of Coleridge now usurps the poem. Playing regretfully with a fancy, Wordsworth speculates that Coleridge's disastrous Cambridge career might have been different had the two friends overlapped as undergraduates. But what might have been only moves Wordsworth because of what is. When these lines were written Coleridge seemed to be breaking up under the pressure of domestic misery, ill-health, drug-addiction, and self-contempt. The Coleridge who had left the Lakes in 1804 to seek health in the Mediterranean had been a ghastly simulacrum of the poet whom Wordsworth addresses at the end of Book II as a fellow-worker in love, 'The most intense of Nature's worshippers' (477). The autobiographical poem was always meant for Coleridge. But now, given his state, it seems more than ever imperative that it should be completed in the fullest possible way:

> Throughout this narrative,
> Else sooner ended, I have known full well
> For whom I thus record the birth and growth
> Of gentleness, simplicity, and truth,
> And joyous loves that hallow innocent days
> Of peace and self-command.
>
> (269–74)

Wordsworth's life must speak to Coleridge's need.

A second, more compelling example of the overlay of present on past occurs at 525–48, which bisects the account of the crossing of the Alps. In 1790 Wordsworth and his walking companion, Robert Jones, were in search of intensity as they hurried on, guide-book in hand, towards the Alps. Both were familiar with mountains, but the peaks of the Lake District and Wales could only hint at what was to be found in the Alps – the ultimate experience of the Sublime.

Their first glimpse of Mont Blanc sets up the tension which dominates the narrative to come:

> That day we first
> Beheld the summit of Mont Blanc, and grieved
> To have a soulless image on the eye
> Which had usurped upon a living thought
> That never more could be. The wondrous Vale
> Of Chamouny did, on the following dawn,
> With its dumb cataracts and streams of ice –
> A motionless array of mighty waves,
> Five rivers broad and vast – make rich amends,
> And reconciled us to realities.
>
> (452–61)

The first five lines of this passage are frequently quoted, but the whole needs to be registered, for this is a declaration of disappointment *and* reconciliation. The imagination, naturalised and thus checked by the real Mont Blanc, is released again by the potentiality of 'dumb cataracts', 'streams of ice' and a 'motionless array of mighty waves'.

At the climax of their experience the same dynamic is enacted. Wordsworth and Jones are in a company of travellers toiling upwards along the road that leads over the Alps to Italy. Lingering over a meal, the pair are separated from their guide and when they set off they naturally take the steepest path forwards, believing that they still have some way to go before they have conquered the Alps. When a stranger tells them, however, that they must retrace their steps, for they have already crossed the Alps, deep dejection overwhelms them. What they had hoped to experience in full consciousness has slipped by, unnoticed. And yet what they came for, they find, not on the peak, but in their descent of the Ravine of Gondo:

> The brook and road
> Were fellow-travellers in this gloomy pass,
> And with them did we journey several hours
> At a slow step. The immeasurable height

Of woods decaying, never to be decayed,
The stationary blasts of waterfalls,
And everywhere along the hollow rent
Winds thwarting winds, bewildered and forlorn,
The torrents shooting from the clear blue sky,
The rocks that muttered close upon our ears –
Black drizzling crags that spake by the wayside
As if a voice were in them – the sick sight
And giddy prospect of the raving stream,
The unfettered clouds and region of the heavens,
Tumult and peace, the darkness and the light,
Were all like workings of one mind, the features
Of the same face, blossoms upon one tree,
Characters of the great apocalypse,
The types and symbols of eternity,
Of first, and last, and midst, and without end.

(553–72)

The passage assaults the senses as do Turner's great Alpine paintings, *The Passage of the St. Gothard* and *The Great Falls of the Reichenbach* (both illustrated in Jonathan Wordsworth, Michael C. Jaye and Robert Woof, *William Wordsworth and the Age of English Romanticism*). Blue sky and black crags, decaying woods that never decay, winds thwarting winds – here every element in Nature works to create what Keats called the 'material sublime'.

The elements also speak of God. In a letter to his sister, Dorothy, actually written while on his Swiss tour, the young Wordsworth had declared that 'Among the more awful scenes of the Alps . . . my whole soul was turned to him who produced the terrible majesty before me' (6 and 16 September 1790). It is a conventionally pious (which does not imply insincere) utterance. The language of *The Prelude*, however, is much more suggestive. According to Thomas Burnet's *Sacred Theory of the Earth* (1681–89), read by both Coleridge and Wordsworth, mountains, seas, and barren places were the direct result of God's act. Once the earth had been fair, smooth, harmonious, but God's judgement on evil men at the time of Noah, the Deluge, had broken the world's frame apart, transforming it to its present state. And so, after this Apocalypse, which means literally Revelation, the world remains, awaiting the final Apocalypse which will herald the end of all things and the Day of Judgement. All aspects of the scene so energetically rendered in this passage are the record, as it were the written 'characters', of God's most awesome demonstration of his power.

Whatever Wordsworth experienced in 1790, however, pales before what happens at the moment of writing, when memory is most fully engaged. Wordsworth encounters directly his own power and is over-mastered by it. Between the narrative of the crossing of the Alps and descending the ravine, Wordsworth dramatically inserts an address to his own Imagination, as a power which usurps his consciousness. And it is here, 'in such visitings / Of awful promise, when the light of sense / Goes out in flashes that have shewn to us / The invisible world' (533–6), that Wordsworth locates the true Sublime. 'Blest in thoughts / That are their own perfection and reward' (545–6), the mind outsoars the material sublime with glimpses of infinitude. The address to Imagination is the poem's first statement of, and a dramatic embodiment of, the great declaration about the Mind of Man with which *The Prelude* is to conclude.

But this is not Blake. 'Imagination has nothing to do with Memory,' he said, in his annotations to Wordsworth's *Poems* of 1815. And again, 'Natural Objects always did & now do Weaken deaden & obliterate Imagination in Me'. On the contrary Wordsworth insists, and continues to insist throughout *The Prelude*, Imagination has everything to do with Memory and Natural Objects. The visible world is its sphere; Memory is its agent. Imagination is greater than either and transcends both. It gives glimpses of 'The invisible world' (536), but its ground is this one.

'Blank confusion', 'Beauteous the domain': Books VII and VIII

The book on London, VII, and the discursive one on the topic 'Love of Nature Leading to Love of Mankind', VIII, are a problem. The difficulty is not their structure, nor their theme, but the fact that what is actually going on in the poetry everywhere subverts, and at times threatens to overwhelm, the explicitly stated structure and theme.

Structurally the two books form a unit made up of parallels and contrasts. In VII the poet, now a 'casual dweller and at large' (61) pitches his 'vagrant tent' (60) in London, a transient, with a house but not a home (76–7). A gazetteer of the sights of the capital city follows, its buildings, gardens, tradesmen and traffic, mountebanks, foreigners, actors, lawyers, politicians, and clerics, which culminates in a frantic evocation of the 'anarchy and din / Barbarian and infernal' (660–1) of the St Bartholomew's Fair. Book VIII opens with another fair, but this time it is situated in the Lake District in the fields below Helvellyn, the mountain that dominates the mass north-east of Grasmere. The people are few, 'a little family of men – / Twice twenty – with their children and their wives' (7–8) and their greetings, gossip, and bargaining scarcely disturbs the quiet of the vale. These are people at home, knowing each other as members of a community, and it is their lives which the rest of the book celebrates. In conclusion the poet returns to London and re-assesses how one might make sense of its seemingly endless variety.

Thematically, too, Books VII and VIII seem to cohere:

> How often in the overflowing streets
> Have I gone forwards with the crowd, and said
> Unto myself, 'The face of every one
> That passes by me is a mystery'.

(595–8)

This, essentially, is the text for Book VII. An outsider, Wordsworth parades before us the spectacles of the city, struggling to get a purchase on its multitudinousness. But though he can see, he cannot read. The city remains unknowable. A blind beggar 'propped against a wall, upon his chest / Wearing a written paper, to explain / The story of the man, and who he was' (613–15) becomes an emblem of all the multitude in this 'blank confusion' (696). Book VIII, by contrast, presents a knowable community. The villagers beneath Helvellyn know each other and, as a type, are known by the poet. No label is needed to tell him of the life of the shepherds. 'How little they, they and their doings, seem' (50) compared to the immensity of the landscape by which they are embraced, yet theirs, for all its hardship, is the true life. The denizens of the Helvellyn Fair know and belong to their world and it is they, in all their apparent littleness, whom the poet loves.

Structurally and thematically coherent — so from this summary account Books VII and VIII might sound. But difficulties arise once one abandons the summary — which broadly conveys Wordsworth's intention — for the verse itself.

The treatment of London presents two problems. The first is a question of tone. At the beginning of Book VII Wordsworth confesses that like any other provincial youth he had thrilled to the very names of London's magic places, and for much of the book the verse suggests that when he got there he was not disappointed. The Dickensian vigour and inventiveness with which he details the sights, sounds, and people, convey not only a sense of life in itself, but also the quickening of the poet's imagination. Even St Bartholomew's Fair, which, it is claimed, 'lays, / If any spectacle on earth can do, / The whole creative powers of man asleep' (653–5) arouses the poet to vivid observation. Try as he may to assert that all this variety deadened him, the verse says something else.

And in this tension lies a clue, perhaps, to the second problem with the treatment of London, which is that of making sense of what Wordsworth explicitly claims. Repeatedly he presents the city as a threat to Imagination, and so ultimately as a threat to the poet's identity, but at the end of Book VII he unexpectedly declares that

> It is not wholly so to him who looks
> In steadiness, who hath among least things
> An under-sense of greatest, sees the parts
> As parts, but with a feeling of the whole.
>
> (710–13)

The word 'under-sense' is a characteristic Wordsworth coinage, variants of which occur throughout *The Prelude*:

'Under-Powers' (I, 163), 'under-soul' (III, 540), 'under-countenance' (VI, 236), 'under-thirst' (VI, 489), 'under-presence' (XIII, 71). In every case, by the suggestion of space, levels, and hierarchy, Wordsworth gropes to convey his sense of something permanent beneath the superficial shows of life. So it is here. Steadied by 'The mountain's outline and its steady form' (723), the poet survives the city's onslaught intact. At the end of Book VIII he concedes just that. Here, in the city, he says,

> imagination also found
> An element that pleased her, tried her strength
> Among new objects, simplified, arranged,
> Impregnated my knowledge, made it live
>
> (797–800)

which is exactly what, for all the statements to the contrary, the verse of Book VII suggests.

Book VIII presents a rather different problem. Book VIII has a project – to demonstrate Love of Nature leading to Love of Mankind. And this is clearly a very important project for *The Prelude*. The poem so far has dealt with the growth of an individual consciousness exclusively. Its most significant moments have been moments of intense, private experience. But Wordsworth's whole poetic mission was built on the conviction not only that the poet was 'a man speaking to men', but that he was a man among men, able to bear witness to the truth voiced in *The Old Cumberland Beggar* that 'we have all of us one human heart'. Tracing the development of his poetic imagination, Wordsworth needs to demonstrate that its growth involved the embrace of other human beings, that its power stemmed not from solipsistic self-communing but from its human centredness. Only such a poet could hope to write a 'philosophic song / Of truth that cherishes our daily life' (I, 230–1).

The difficulty with Book VIII, however, is not that this thesis is inherently implausible (though many will think that it is) but that there is a disjunction between what Wordsworth asserts as thesis and what he offers as supporting evidence. The argument is stated in expository verse at 69–80, 178–221, 410–16, 428–71, and recapitulated at 587–9:

> My present theme
> Is to retrace the way that led me on
> Through Nature to the love of human-kind.

None of the illustrative material, however, supports this as a general and inclusive proposition. Wordsworth certainly declares that he loved shepherds from his earliest days, but in suggesting why he found them heroic beings, the verse repeatedly discloses the activity of Wordsworth's literary imagination, so much so that one might infer that the truer thesis would be, 'Love of Books leading to Love of Humankind'. Only in the interpolated 'Matron's Tale' (222–311) – material discarded from *Michael*, a blank verse narrative published in *Lyrical Ballads*, 1800 – does Wordsworth look steadily at a Lake District shepherd. As with all Wordsworth's exemplary tales, especially in *The Excursion*, he presents it baldly, as if a narrative of a human life is in itself beyond all commentary. But what 'The Matron's Tale' demonstrates is the intensity of the poet's feeling for 'Man suffering among awful powers and forms' (213), his love for the inhabitants of his particular nook of earth, not that Nature had led him to anything as grand as Loving Humankind.

'Bliss was it in that dawn to be alive': Books IX and X

Books IX and X, which cover the poet's development from the age of twenty-one to twenty-six, are fascinating. But they are also denser than any of the previous books and the student should not be discouraged if even after repeated readings much remains unclear.

Wordsworth deploys a great deal of material in these books and what he wants to do with it inevitably makes for difficulties. The basic narrative line is this. The poet goes to France late in 1791, two years after the beginning of the French Revolution. Whereas in 1790 Wordsworth had hurried through France *en route* for the Alps, now he intends to live there. He begins by visiting all the notable places in Paris, but admits that he was no more than a tourist, 'Affecting more emotion than I felt' (IX, 71). During his year's residence in provincial France, however, he becomes a fervent supporter of the Revolution − 'my heart was all / Given to the people, and my love was theirs' (XI, 124–5). When Wordsworth returns to Paris late in 1792 France has become a Republic, but one stained in the blood of the September massacres and riven by the factional in-fighting fomented by Robespierre. The poet's faith remains strong, however, so much so that he returns to England expecting to find a like spirit in his countrymen. He is utterly wrong and the outbreak of war between France and England in 1793 isolates him. The fall of Robespierre in July 1794 quickens Wordsworth's hopes again:

> In the people was my trust
> And in the virtues which mine eyes had seen,
> And to the ultimate repose of things
> I looked with unabated confidence.
>
> (X, 577–80)

But this trust proves illusory as the French, 'losing sight of all / Which they had struggled for', (X, 791–2), begin a war of conquest. Shaken by events in France, appalled by the repressive measures against sedition enacted at home, the poet clings more tenaciously to this faith:

> rouzed up, I stuck
> More firmly to old tenets, and to prove
> Their temper, strained them more; and thus, in heat
> Of contest, did opinions every day
> Grow into consequence, till round my mind
> They clung as if they were the life of it.
>
> (X, 799–804)

A crisis now follows. The exposition is not detailed, but Wordsworth seems to suggest that in his zeal to establish his opinions he becomes embroiled in political controversy, testing argument against argument, seeking *proof*, until 'Sick, wearied out with contrarieties' (X, 899) he abandons the pursuit of certitude, having reached an impasse. From this labyrinth of despair he is rescued by the human ministrations of Dorothy

and by 'Nature's self, by human love / Assisted' (X, 921–2).
He closes Book X restored to 'my true self' (915).

Two minor difficulties in this narrative present themselves
to readers. The first is that it demands, as no other part of
The Prelude does, historical knowledge. Wordsworth refers
to 'those September massacres' (X, 64), to Robespierre,
Louvet, Madame Roland, to the anti-slavery campaign (X,
201–10), to the 'confederated host' (X, 230) of the allies
against France, to the fall of Louis XVI (X, 8–10) and so on.
A passing reference invokes but does not detail 'What in
those days through Britain was performed / To turn *all*
judgements out of their right course' (X, 638–9). He means
the severe measures taken against sedition – the suspension
of Habeas Corpus, the 'Gagging Acts' which stifled political
discussion, the 1794 Treason Trials, the army of paid spies
and informers, one of whom even sent reports back to the
Home Office about Wordsworth and Coleridge at Alfoxden.
For a full understanding of the text the reader will need to go
beyond the notes to the Norton edition of *The Prelude* at least
to Albert Goodwin's *The Friends of Liberty* and Nicholas
Roe's *Wordsworth and Coleridge: The Radical Years*.

The second difficulty arises from Wordsworth's attempt in
these books to maintain a dual perspective on his material.
Writing ten years after the event, he believes (a) that he was
lured into a crisis in which he lost touch with his true self; (b)
that the French have betrayed their cause and that there is no
shame in being, now, an English patriot. But Wordsworth
continues to believe, and fervently, (a) that his youthful zeal
for the Revolution was generous and right; (b) that in many
respects his faith in the ideas of the Revolution remains un-
dimmed; (c) that British politicians have been guilty men
throughout 'ten shameful years' (X, 178). The result is that
throughout these books the focus constantly shifts between a
vivid chronicle of events in the early 1790s and reflective,
expository verse such as X, 380–439, in which the poet seeks
to explain his frame of mind then from the vantage point of
now. The passage beginning 'Bliss was it in that dawn to be
alive, / But to be young was very heaven!' (X, 692–735) is

another example of dual-perspective, which calls for close attention to nuance and tone.

The main narrative, the sequential chronicle of Wordsworth's development, presents no difficulties, however, for it is finely orchestrated around four climaxes. The first is the moment when the poet's unfocussed idealism becomes a passion. In Blois Wordsworth's understanding of French politics was deepened, and given edge, by a passionate friendship with Michel Beaupuy, who is the subject of a lengthy tribute at IX, 294–347. Out walking with his mentor, Michel Beaupuy, Wordsworth sees a hunger-bitten girl leading a heifer:

> at the sight my friend
> In agitation said, ''Tis against that
> Which we are fighting', I with him believed
> Devoutly that a spirit was abroad
> Which could not be withstood, that poverty,
> At least like this, would in a little time
> Be found no more.
>
> (IX, 518–24)

The second climax is when Britain declares war on France in 1793. This 'unnatural strife' (X, 250) ravages the poet's heart. Just how deeply is conveyed in this terrible image of isolation:

> It was a grief –
> Grief call it not, 'twas anything but that –
> A conflict of sensations without name,
> Of which he only who may love the sight
> Of a village steeple as I do can judge,
> When in the congregation, bending all
> To their great Father, prayers were offered up
> Or praises for our country's victories,
> And, 'mid the simple worshippers perchance
> I only, like an uninvited guest
> Whom no one owned, sate silent – shall I add,
> Fed on the day of vengeance yet to come!
>
> (X, 263–74)

There is ample evidence that this is not a hyperbolic recollection of how he felt in 1793. The prose *Letter to the Bishop*

of Llandaff, written shortly after the declaration of war, and
Salisbury Plain, written over the following year, are marked
by considerable violence and a tone of controlled fury. (For
the *Letter* see the Owen and Smyser edition of Wordsworth's
prose; for *Salisbury Plain* see the *Oxford Authors: Wordsworth*, ed. Stephen Gill or the *Cornell Wordsworth* volume,
The Salisbury Plain Poems of William Wordsworth (Ithaca,
1975), same editor.) Wordsworth published neither work,
very sensibly, for both were undoubtedly seditious.

The third is the climax of hope restored. Staying on the
southern edge of the Lake District in 1794, far from London
and the political centre, Wordsworth hears in a casual conversation that Robespierre is dead. Spontaneously he pours out
'A hymn of triumph' (X, 539–66), confident that the earth
would now 'March firmly towards righteousness and peace'.

The final one is the poet's nadir, already quoted on p. 35.
Here the verse powerfully enacts his torment as he struggles
to reach truth through mistaken means, his reasonings being
false 'From the beginning, inasmuch as drawn / Out of a
heart which had been turned aside / From Nature by external
accidents, / And which was thus confounded more and more,
/ Misguiding and misguided' (X, 883–7).

If the narrative as such presents no problems in reading
other than the ones already mentioned, there are nonetheless
two aspects of it that need to be discussed. The first is that
Wordsworth has omitted a significant part of his experience,
namely that in France he fathered a child on Annette Vallon,
that he was driven to separate from her while he went back
home to look for money and employment, and that the outbreak of the war enforced the separation which became permanent. By the time he was writing *The Prelude* Wordsworth
was married to Mary Hutchinson.

None of this biographical material, perhaps, demands
inclusion in an account of the growth of a poet's mind,
although many will feel that fathering a child only to be
separated from its mother before the baby is born, must have
a considerable impact on anyone's emotional and imaginative
development. But if it is to be omitted as irrelevant to the

concerns of this poem, one might think it should be omitted altogether. Instead Wordsworth interpolates the tale of Vaudracour and Julia (IX, 556–935), a story of two lovers crushed by the powers of family and state. The story is presented as a substitute for 'other matters which detained us oft / In thought or conversation' (X, 545–6), but it is a poor substitute. Presented without comment, in *The Prelude*'s flattest verse, it lies inert, revealing less than it promises either about the family, law, and politics in France, or about Wordsworth's experience of sexual passion and the responsibilities it entails.

'Vaudracour and Julia' is a problem, but not one about which it is difficult to have a view. The second aspect of these books I want to discuss, however, is altogether more interesting. It concerns Wordsworth's 'crisis'.

What caused and what was the nature of the intellectual-emotional-moral implosion depicted so strikingly in Book X? The poem's main propositions are clear enough (however unsettlingly vague some of the language and the chronological pointing): betrayed by the course of the Revolution and isolated from the mood of his own country, Wordsworth returned to fundamentals, 'To think with fervour upon management / Of nations – what is and ought to be, / And how their worth depended on their laws, / And on the constitution of the state' (X, 685–8). What attracted most was any philosophy that 'promised to abstract the hopes of man / Out of his feelings, to be fixed thenceforth / For ever in a purer element' (X, 807–9), such a philosophy, for example, as that expounded by the rationalist William Godwin in *An Enquiry Concerning Political Justice* (1793). The pursuit of such 'secure intelligence' (X, 833), that is, of abstract certainties, led only to perplexity so total that the poet abandoned 'moral questions', turning to mathematics 'and their clear / And solid evidence' (X, 893–4) as a prophylactic against complete mental breakdown. Various agencies, however, 'Maintained for me a saving intercourse / With my true self' (X, 914–15), and the poet emerges from his crisis, like the moon when obscuring clouds pass by (X, 917).

As a narrative of cause and effect this is clear and not implausible, but there is no evidence that, *as the poem presents
it*, it is true to what actually happened in Wordsworth's life.
He was certainly engaged politically, both in his own writing
and in discussion with radical friends, but nowhere in his letters, or in the letters and memoirs of others, is there any
evidence that Wordsworth ever 'yielded up moral questions in
despair'. Again, Wordsworth certainly read Godwin and was
for a while a frequent visitor to his house, but all of the
available evidence suggests that the influence on him of
Political Justice was short-lived. Nor does anything substantiate the picture of Wordsworth retiring from politics to the
countryside where he was nursed back to health. Wordsworth
went to Dorset by the mere chance that he needed accom-
modation and a friend offered it rent-free; he did not 'give
up' politics at Racedown or Alfoxden, that is, he kept up with
reading, writing, and radical friends; in Dorset his friends,
especially his new friend Coleridge, found him markedly
energetic and productive. No one refers to him as a convales-
cent. (For a fuller treatment of this period, and evidence for
these assertions, see my biography already mentioned, pp.
94–155.)

So why for *The Prelude* does Wordsworth so persuasively
elaborate a myth of crisis and fall? Two speculative answers
may be offered. The first is that in Books IX and X Wordsworth was dramatising what he now, in 1804–5, perceived
to be the great truth about himself as a man and as a poet,
namely that by 1797, the end of his period at Racedown, he
had come through. Ever since Cambridge Wordsworth had
been homeless, unemployed, directionless, at odds with his
family. Though he had written a lot, he had published almost
nothing and certainly could not claim any public reputation
as a writer. What he had composed since 1793 had been
overtly political and even at Racedown a new poem, *Adventures on Salisbury Plain*, was described as being designed to
'exhibit the vices of the penal law'. By the time he left
Racedown, however, overt political engagement had receded.
Not only had he begun to write in the manner of the 'Great

Decade' on which his reputation rests, but he was ready within months to join Coleridge in a plan for a philosophical poem that would explore fundamental truths about 'Nature, Man, and Society' (letter, 6 March 1798). All of the turbulent experiences of life and politics had in some way − he did not quite know how − cohered. And with that coherence came the massive confidence (which some acquaintances later reacted to as a daunting egotism) that he *knew* now that he was meant to be a poet and that in the light of this knowledge all of his previous life made sense. He was a 'chosen son'.

The second speculation arises out of this last sentence. It is that Wordsworth telescopes many years of disparate experience into one dramatic narrative of crisis and fall because the economy of *The Prelude* demands it. The whole of the poem is structured to affirm that its creator was ordained to be a poet of a particular kind, one possessed of certain truths about the ultimate realities − Nature, God, Man, Imagination. So far the poem has traced the evolution of Imagination and has asserted the fundamental value that the Imagination, fostered by Nature, will embrace Humankind. But what the poet has not yet done is show Imagination tested in any serious way in life's wider possible engagements, nor demonstrate love of Humankind in action. The account of Wordsworth's commitment to human ideals at the moment of the Revolution, and of his subsequent loss of faith in *political* activity as a means of furthering them, does both. By revealing both what the poet's Imagination did embrace and what it was ultimately baffled by, Books IX and X open the way for the sustained affirmation of what kind of poet Wordsworth is that makes up the remainder of the poem.

'A saving intercourse': Books XI and XIII

Books XI and XII have both a similar structure. In both, peaks of visionary poetry dominate extensive foothills of lack-lustre expository verse. In each case the visionary, it is claimed, illustrates and validates the expository, but if it does so at all, it is strangely and obliquely. That is, the poetry works, as all of Wordsworth's greatest and most characteristic poetry does, through indirection.

Book XI opens with a paean to Nature and a return to the 'breezes and soft airs' (10) welcomed in the poem's opening lines. The poet then reflects on the effect his spiritual crisis had on his relationship with Nature, 'all the sources of [his] former strength' (77), on the destructive power of reason if incautiously employed, and on the danger of rule-dominated aesthetic judgement of Nature, such as the cult of the picturesque. But Wordsworth's heart seems not to be in his task. Twice, at 120–35 and 175–84, he introduces major issues, only to evade them by declaring that 'this is matter for another song' (184).

At line 257, however, this dull and rather directionless book is transformed by two moments of visionary poetry which demonstrate, the poet avers, that after his long travail his was, and now still is, 'A sensitive and a *creative* soul' (256). A preamble highlights the significance of the episodes that are to follow:

> There are in our existence spots of time,
> Which with distinct preeminence retain
> A renovating virtue, whence, depressed
> By false opinion and contentious thought,
> Or aught of heavier or more deadly weight
> In trivial occupations and the round
> Of ordinary intercourse, our minds
> Are nourished and invisibly repaired.
>
> (XI, 257–64)

Then comes the 'Woman on Penrith Beacon' (278–327) and, after a transition passage, the 'Waiting for the Horses' (344–88). The whole sequence is discussed with exemplary care by David Ellis in *Wordsworth, Freud and the Spots of Time*.

Although the history of Wordsworth's development has reached his mid-twenties by Book XI, the 'Spots of Time' look back to his early childhood. In the first the boy, 'not six years old' (279), is separated from the family servant while out riding. Lost and increasingly scared, he stumbles into a valley bottom, where a murderer once hung in chains on the gibbet. The climax to the episode is an epiphany:

> forthwith I left the spot,
> And, reascending the bare common, saw
> A naked pool that lay beneath the hills,
> The beacon on the summit, and more near,
> A girl who bore a pitcher on her head
> And seemed with difficult steps to force her way
> Against the blowing wind. It was, in truth,
> An ordinary sight, but I should need
> Colours and words that are unknown to man
> To paint the visionary dreariness
> Which, while I looked all round for my lost guide,
> Did at that time invest the naked pool,
> The beacon on the lonely eminence,
> The woman, and her garments vexed and tossed
> By the strong wind.

(XI, 301–15)

In the second 'Spot of Time' the thirteen-year-old boy is waiting in the hills outside Hawkshead to catch a glimpse of the horses sent to carry the Wordsworth brothers home from school for Christmas:

> 'Twas a day
> Stormy, and rough, and wild, and on the grass
> I sate half-sheltered by a naked wall.
> Upon my right hand was a single sheep,
> A whistling hawthorn on my left, and there,
> With those companions at my side, I watched,
> Straining my eyes intensely as the mist
> Gave intermitting prospect of the wood
> And plain beneath.

(XI, 355–63)

Within ten days Wordsworth's father is dead. The child responds to the pain and sense of abandonment in a familiar way – by blaming himself for having indulged in 'such anxiety of hope' (371). What the boy remembers most vividly, however, becomes a continuing source of consolation and strength:

> And afterwards the wind and sleety rain,
> And all the business of the elements,

The single sheep, and the one blasted tree,
And the bleak music of that old stone wall,
The noise of wood and water, and the mist
Which on the line of each of those two roads
Advanced in such indisputable shapes –
All these were spectacles and sounds to which
I often would repair, and thence would drink
As at a fountain.

(XI, 375–84)

Both of these incidents are, in the richest sense of the word, mysterious. What actually happened to the boy can never be known, but whatever it was, it impressed upon his mind certain images which yield themselves up each time memory interrogates the event – the 'ordinary sight' of the woman on the lonely eminence, her clothes flapping in the wind, the dry-stone wall, the single sheep, and the hawthorn tree. These bleak fundamentals are imaged as nourishment. In *Tintern Abbey* a moment of rich experience promises 'food / For future years' (65–6). Here the memories give life as water from a fountain (eighteenth-century usage for a spring).

The 'Spots of Time' were written for the *Two-Part Prelude* of 1799 (I, 288–374), where they fit into a series of examples of experiences which illustrate 'the growth of natural power / And love of Nature's works' (I, 257–8). They are highlighted as especially powerful spots of time, but given that their context is all the other episodes of childhood, the birds'-nesting, skating, and so on, they do not appear to have a different function in the *Two-Part Prelude* from these other incidents. By extracting them from the account of childhood, however, to place them in Book XI of the 1805 *Prelude*, Wordsworth endows them with a special significance. What saved him in his crisis, the poet declares in Book X, were agencies which 'Maintained for me a saving intercourse / With my true self' (914–15). In Book XI the 'Spots of Time' affirm this saving intercourse. Repairing to the fountains of these memories, the poet returns to the origins of his strength. The whole passage affirms what is elsewhere presented as a life-giving paradox:

> The Child is Father of the Man;
> And I could wish my days to be
> Bound each to each by natural piety.
>
> ('My heart leaps up . . .')

At this moment of affirmation, however, the poet discloses a counter-spirit of anxiety. The *Two-Part Prelude* had asserted with confidence that the memory of such moments creates for the mind forms and images 'That yet exist with independent life, / And, like their archetypes, know no decay' (I, 286–7). The 1805 *Prelude* puts the emphasis differently. In the transition passage (XI, 328–44), which belongs to the 1804 composition and not to the 1799 *Prelude*, Wordsworth suggests that in the creative, reciprocal activity of Imagination and material, of Memory and event, some diminution is to be feared, to which poetry, the product of the Imagination, is the surest check:

> The days gone by
> Come back upon me from the dawn almost
> Of life; the hiding-places of my power
> Seem open, I approach, and then they close;
> I see by glimpses now, when age comes on
> May scarcely see at all; and I would give
> While yet we may, as far as words can give,
> A substance and life to what I feel:
> *I would enshrine the spirit of the past*
> *For future restoration.*
>
> (My italics)

These lines, especially those italicised, mark out the crucial difference between the 'Spots of Time' in 1799 and in the 1804–5 *Prelude*. In the *Two-Part Prelude* it is memory alone which is hymned as the saving power. Now Wordsworth emphasises the role of poetry. It is words which must 'enshrine' the spirit of the past and act as a counter-spirit to the process of decay.

In Book XII likewise it is a passage of visionary poetry which focusses the exposition. Recapitulating the stages of his recovery – 'On all sides day began to reappear' (22) – Wordsworth declares that renewed contact with Nature and his own true self led him to find 'Once more in man an object

of delight, / Of pure imagination, and of love' (54–5). A
lengthy passage follows (69–219) about the nature of dignity
and worth, which ends in a declaration, complementary to the
Preface to *Lyrical Ballads* (1800), as to why the poet has
chosen to dwell on simple men and rural themes. It rests upon
the conviction that,

> Nature through all conditions hath a power
> To consecrate – if we have eyes to see –
> The outside of her creatures, and to breathe
> Grandeur upon the very humblest face
> Of human life.

(XII, 282–6)

This is to be Wordsworth's theme. His hope is that he might
become one of the mighty band of poets 'enabled to perceive
/ Something unseen before' (304–5) and that his poetry

> Proceeding from the depth of untaught things,
> Enduring and creative, might become
> A power like one of Nature's.

(310–12)

What illustrates this exposition is quite unexpected. One
might have anticipated another encounter, such as that with
the Discharged Soldier in Book IV (360–504), or another tale
of rural life, such as 'The Matron's Tale' of Book VIII
(222–311), both of which celebrate 'Man suffering among
awful powers and forms' (VIII, 213). What Book XII offers
instead is an account of Wordsworth's vision as he crossed
Salisbury Plain (312–53).

In 1793 Wordsworth had watched the British fleet preparing for war off the Isle of Wight, convinced, as he later recalled, that the 'struggle which was beginning . . . would be
of long continuance, and productive of distress and misery
beyond all possible calculation' ('Advertisement' to *Guilt and
Sorrow*, published 1842). Leaving the coast, he set off for a
tour of the West Country with a friend, but an accident to
their carriage ended the excursion and Wordsworth set off
alone to walk across Salisbury Plain, making for South
Wales. His actual isolation heightened by a sense of being a
stranger in his own country, the poet was clearly in a

tormented state as he ranged through 'those vestiges of ancient times' (318). Overcome by the solitude, he had

> a reverie and saw the past,
> Saw multitudes of men, and here and there
> A single Briton in his wolf-skin vest,
> With shield and stone-ax, stride across the wold.
>
> (XII, 320–3)

At other times, inspecting the evidences of Druidic knowledge surviving in the 'Lines, circles, mounts' (340) on the Plain, Wordsworth

> saw the bearded teachers, with white wands
> Uplifted, pointing to the starry sky,
> Alternately, and plain below, while breath
> Of music seemed to guide them, and the waste
> Was cheered with stillness and a pleasant sound.
>
> (XII, 349–53)

This is a particularly interesting moment in the poem. In a work intended for Coleridge's eyes, Wordsworth narrates an experience he had before he ever met him. As he does so, he quotes directly (in the passages above) from what he wrote immediately after the experience in 1793, *Salisbury Plain*, a poem which Coleridge valued highly and to which he pays a striking tribute in *Biographia Literaria*. It was, says Coleridge, one of the achievements which made him realise first that Wordsworth was a writer of more than common power. In *Salisbury Plain*, however, the Druids serve to heighten the projection of a political denunciation. Their human sacrifices and obeisance to superstition are analogies, the poem asserts, to the present-day sacrifice of human life enacted by the evil partnership of State and Church. The poem concludes with an appeal to the 'Heroes of Truth' to continue their work of destruction until nothing is left of Superstition's reign, 'Save that eternal pile which frowns on Sarum's plain'.

In *The Prelude* the function of the Druids is very different. Any connection between them and rural man is remote, but their connection to the poet is clear. Wordsworth now images them as ministrants of power, alternately pointing to the sky and to the earth. What he is celebrating here is the poet's capacity to make what he will from all materials — the power of Imagination. And the Salisbury Plain passage itself is an example of how that power typically operates in Wordsworth's poetry. Returning in memory to a formative experience, Wordsworth also returns to the poetry which inscribed that experience and reinterprets it, rewriting it in response to current preoccupations. The whole sequence serves as an introduction to the concerns of Book XIII.

The 'Mighty Mind': Book XIII

Manuscript evidence suggests that in all of the structures Wordsworth contemplated for the poem after the 1799 *Two-Part Prelude*, it was intended that the Climbing of Snowdon should be the climax. Justifiably so, for the description of the ascent (1–65) and the subsequent meditation (66–199) join beautifully together to make this both the poem's richest example of Imagination at work and its fullest exposition of the significance of this creative power.

As with the crossing of the Alps, Wordsworth begins his narrative with homely details of time, place, and circumstance. He and his alpine companion, Robert Jones, want to climb Snowdon to see the sun rise. To the east are the mountains and lower hills of North Wales, to the west the Irish Sea. They rouse a mountain guide and set off, travellers' chat soon lapsing into silence as for an hour or more they labour upwards. There is a sense of expectation, but not of the unknown. Wordsworth and Jones know exactly what it is they want to see. But their expectation is overset by a completely unexpected display. Paraphrase is no substitute for this, some of the finest blank verse Wordsworth ever wrote. As they toil up in the darkness,

> at my feet the ground appeared to brighten,
> And with a step or two seemed brighter still;
> Nor had I time to ask the cause of this,
> For instantly a light upon the turf
> Fell like a flash. I looked about, and lo,
> The moon stood naked in the heavens at height

Immense above my head, and on the shore
I found myself of a huge sea of mist,
Which meek and silent rested at my feet.
A hundred hills their dusky backs upheaved
All over this still ocean, and beyond,
Far, far beyond, the vapours shot themselves
In headlands, tongues, and promontory shapes,
Into the sea, the real sea, that seemed
To dwindle and give up its majesty,
Usurped upon as far as sight could reach.
Meanwhile, the moon looked down upon this shew
In single glory, and we stood, the mist
Touching our very feet; and from the shore
At distance not the third part of a mile
Was a blue chasm, a fracture in the vapour,
A deep and gloomy breathing-place, through which
Mounted the roar of waters, torrents, streams
Innumerable, roaring with one voice.

(XIII, 36–59)

Throughout *The Prelude* Wordsworth has traced the growth of Imagination. Now, in the meditation that follows the ascent, he celebrates in tones of awed reverence but absolute confidence what its properties are. In the amazing spectacle on the mountain Nature has presented an analogy to Imagination by exerting on the 'outward face of things' (78) her power to 'mould', 'endue', 'abstract', 'combine' (79). Such a power is that of truly creative minds:

This is the very spirit in which they deal
With all the objects of the universe:
They from their native selves can send abroad
Like transformation, for themselves create
A like existence, and, when'er it is
Created for them, catch it by an instinct.
Them the enduring and the transient both
Serve to exalt. They build up greatest things
From least suggestions, ever on the watch,
Willing to work and to be wrought upon.
They need not extraordinary calls
To rouze them – in a world of life they live,
By sensible impressions not enthralled,
But quickened, rouzed, and made thereby more fit
To hold communion with the invisible world.

(XIII, 91–105)

Such minds, the passage concludes, 'are truly from the Deity'
(106).

These lines, only an excerpt from the whole meditation, are
amongst the most important Wordsworth ever wrote and full
commentary on them would invoke in one way or another
most of the dominant concerns of English Romanticism. One
strand of commentary might pursue the relationship between
this meditation and developing concepts of mind and perception. Many of the various conceptions of the mind in the
eighteenth century accepted a model which emphasised the
mind's essential passivity before sensory input. It became, in
Coleridge's phrase, 'a lazy Looker-on on an external World' (letter, 23 March 1801). Wordsworth and Coleridge, to the contrary,
present the mind in perception as vitally active, engaged in a constant act of creation-in-perception. (For a full study of this issue,
see Engell's book on *The Creative Imagination*.)

Another line of commentary might emphasise the
theological implications of the Snowdon meditation. Truly
creative minds, Wordsworth asserts, both are from the Deity
and partake of the nature of Deity. Utterly rejecting the common notion that the world was a well-oiled machine, beautifully constructed by an artificer God, who then left it to operate
according to mechanical laws, Wordsworth and Coleridge
were the first of the Romantics to insist on God's vital engagement in the world and on Man's capacity to know His presence
as energy and power.

One might also follow up the meditation's affirmation of the
supreme importance of the Imagination. One line of enquiry
would lead back to the Preface to *Lyrical Ballads* of 1802,
where Wordsworth declares:

[The poet] is the rock of defence of human nature; an upholder and
preserver, carrying everywhere with him relationship and love. In
spite of difference of soil and climate, of language and manners, of
laws and customs, in spite of things silently gone out of mind and
things violently destroyed, the Poet binds together by passion and
knowledge the vast empire of human society, as it is spread over the
whole earth, and over all time. The objects of the Poet's thoughts
are everywhere; though the eyes and senses of man are, it is true, his
favorite guides, yet he will follow wheresoever he can find an

atmosphere of sensation in which to move his wings. Poetry is the first and last of all knowledge − it is as immortal as the heart of man.

But one would also look forward to Keats and ultimately to Shelley's *Defence of Poetry*, with its ringing conclusion, 'Poets are the unacknowledged legislators of the World'.

Perhaps what needs to be emphasised most of all about the Snowdon meditation, however, is the stress placed on reciprocity and interaction. In the passage printed in 1814 as a 'Prospectus' to *The Recluse* Wordsworth declares that Paradise need not be 'A History, or but a dream', 'when minds / Once wedded to this outward frame of things / In love, find these the growth of common day'. The 'Prospectus' was scornfully rejected by Blake as a deathly subjugation of the autonomous, creative mind, to the palpable realities of matter. But Wordsworth insists on his image of the 'wedding' of the mind and nature. Imagination is the sacred power. 'Willing to work and to be wrought upon', creative minds engage in 'an ennobling interchange / Of action from within and from without' (XII, 375–6). The Snowdon meditation both celebrates the highest power of mind as mind and anchors it in quotidian reality.

For most readers *The Prelude* stops here. But while it is true that there is nothing in the remainder of the poem to match the power of this section, it would be a mistake to regard the rest of Book XIII as in-fill. A meditation on Love as the prime principle of life, inextricable from the highest exercise of Imagination (142–65), leads to a recapitulation of the theme of the whole poem (166–84), and then to a lengthy section in which the poet embraces those whose love has supported and nurtured him. Finally Wordsworth addresses Coleridge once more, recalling the summer in which *Lyrical Ballads* was born:

> When thou dost to that summer turn thy thoughts,
> And hast before thee all which then we were,
> To thee, in memory of that happiness,
> It will be known − by thee at least, my friend,
> Felt − that the history of a poet's mind
> Is labour not unworthy of regard:
> To thee the work shall justify itself.

(404–10)

What Wordsworth is recalling here, and inviting Coleridge to recall, is the moment when they both shared every aspect of life so intimately that joint publication of their poems seemed not just convenient but the only appropriate mode. Then they knew they were of one mind. But 1798 was also the summer in which *The Recluse* was conceived, the philosophical work to which this whole poem is but a prelude. So quite properly Wordsworth concludes with a re-dedication of himself and Coleridge as 'joint labourers' (439) in a work of 'lasting inspiration, sanctified / By reason and by truth' (443–4):

> what we have loved
> Others will love, and we may teach them how:
> Instruct them how the mind of man becomes
> A thousand times more beautiful than the earth
> On which he dwells, above this frame of things
> (Which 'mid all revolutions in the hopes
> And fears of men, doth still remain unchanged)
> In beauty exalted, as it itself
> Of substance and of fabric more divine.
>
> (444–52)

The Prelude opens with a poet who candidly admits that, doubting his own powers, he is evading the great subject. It closes with a welcome to that great task yet to be fulfilled. What *The Prelude* actually demonstrates is that Wordsworth's powers were never in doubt, and that he has completed the most arduous, and the most exciting work he was ever to undertake – an account of the Growth of a Poet's Mind, his own.

Chapter 5

The Prelude since 1850

Reception

Wordsworth died on 23 April 1850 and *The Prelude* was published in July. Two thousand copies were printed and the poem was widely and respectfully reviewed. By 1851 the edition was exhausted and a smaller format, cheaper second edition was issued.

These details need emphasising, because it has become a common-place of literary history that *The Prelude* was a failure. Herbert Lindenberger's assessment that reviewers were lukewarm and the book-buying public unenthusiastic, has been generally accepted ('The Reception of *The Prelude*', *Bulletin of the New York Public Library*, 64 (1960), pp. 196–208). But it is not quite just in its emphasis. Compared with Tennyson's *In Memoriam*, also published in 1850, which went through many thousands of copies and five editions by the end of 1851, *The Prelude* made only a modest show. As Lee Erickson has pointed out, however, 'no single work previous to *The Prelude* had been printed in as large an edition as two thousand copies nor sold as quickly' ('The Egoism of Authorship: Wordsworth's Poetic Career', *Journal of English and Germanic Philology*, 89 (1990), p. 48). While it is true and remarkable that three of the major journals did not notice the poem (*Edinburgh Review, Blackwood's, Quarterly Review*), there were many more reviews than Lindenberger indicated and they were generally positive.

If Lindenberger's argument is shaky in detail, however, his sense that there is something odd about the reception of *The Prelude* is well founded. In fact the poem did not emerge as a major work, if not *the* major work of Wordsworth, until well into the next century. There were, I suggest, three reasons for this delay.

The first is that in 1850 *The Prelude* was a strange, belated phenomenon, intractable material which resisted assimilation into the public image of 'Wordsworth' evolved over fifty years. By the time of his death Wordsworth had been Poet Laureate for seven years, whose recent work included *Ode on the Installation of His Royal Highness Prince Albert as Chancellor of the University of Cambridge* (1847). Unofficial Poet Laureate of the Anglican Church, Wordsworth had lived to see his early poetry re-assessed and absorbed by a later generation, which welcomed what was perceived as its continuity with his later, more avowedly Christian writing. Long esteemed by undoctrinaire Broad Church readers, Wordsworth was even fêted by the High Church party as one whose 'poems did in diverse places anticipate the revival of catholic doctrines among us' (for reference and further details see my *William Wordsworth: A Life*, pp. 417–18.)

The Prelude unsettled this image dramatically. There was no problem with the early books, of course. Their account of childhood experiences of Nature fell into place readily with much of Wordsworth's best-loved work. The treatment of Cambridge must have raised some eyebrows, not least amongst the dons of St John's College, who in 1832 had paid for a portrait of the poet as one of the college's most distinguished alumni, but surprise at Wordsworth's views on his old university was easily tempered by self-congratulation that things had much improved at Cambridge since the 1780s. Wordsworth's narrative of his political odyssey, however, could not be absorbed without shock. Macaulay's 'The poem is to the last degree Jacobinical, indeed Socialist', might have seemed overstated to some, but no one could ignore its core of truth. What *The Prelude* disclosed was that the poet had been an ardent supporter of the French, that he remained unrepentant about his views on British policy in the early 1790s, and that his humanitarian poetry had its base in the ideals he espoused then. Hazlitt's assertion in *The Spirit of the Age* (1825) that Wordsworth's muse was 'a levelling one' took on a deeper, perhaps more sinister, significance. *The Prelude*'s conclusion, moreover, revealed that Wordsworth and Coleridge had had a mission to redeem the world. That the 'work . . . of their redemption, surely yet to come' (XIII, 439–41) operated in the realm of the spirit could not disguise the truth that such a mission was inherently radical.

This Wordsworth, emerging sixty years after the French Revolution, was clearly not the Victorian Poet Laureate, an uncomfortable fact which caused the poet's highly orthodox clerical nephew, Christopher Wordsworth, some difficulty as he wrote his *Memoirs of William Wordsworth*, the 'official biography' published in 1851. For many readers, however, it must have seemed just a fact of history, of little importance now. *In Memoriam*, by contrast, was evidently a poem of the present. Whereas Wordsworth's Natural Theology has its roots in eighteenth-century epistemology, Tennyson engages with the competing discourses of science and theology in a way that commanded the respect of both advanced scientists and churchmen. At a time when religious issues dominated contemporary debate to a degree inconceivable today, *In Memoriam* regained for poetry a central position. Tennyson's poem, in short, was obviously important and contemporary. Wordsworth's looked like a survival from a world of intellectual and political upheaval now thankfully past.

The second reason for the delayed recognition of *The Prelude* is that 'Wordsworth' (the whole phenomenon of the poetry, the message, the personal image) had already been established in the mind of his most influential successors before *The Prelude* appeared. Between 1840 and 1880 Wordsworth's reputation was at its peak, fostered directly by lecturers and essayists who explicated the poetry on occasion as if it were Holy Writ. But the reputation grew also because other writers in their own work indirectly disseminated what might loosely be termed a Wordsworthian ethos. Elizabeth Gaskell quoted at length from *The Old Cumberland Beggar* when trying to explain how her perception that the 'beauty and poetry of many of the common things and daily events of life in its humblest aspect does not seem . . . sufficiently appreciated' was spurring her to write 'sketches among the poor' (letter, 18 August 1838). The young George Eliot absorbed Wordsworth with delight: 'I never before met with so many of my own feelings, expressed just as I could like them' (letter, 22 November 1839) and quotations from the poems throughout her novels point up the continuity between her moral vision and Wordsworth's. It is on record, for example, that Eliot thought Wordsworth would have been the ideal reader of *Silas Marner*. Ruskin, whose impact on mid-Victorian culture is incalculable, was the Wordsworth for his generation. And what all of these writers absorbed was the poet of the lyrics and *The Excursion. The Prelude* simply appeared too late for it to become a shaping factor in their experience as the earlier poetry had been.

The third reason is that the canon and Wordsworth's achievement were being re-assessed and re-presented, in a way that rebuffed the posthumous long poem. In part this was just the result of the practicalities of publishing. Most second-hand bookshops can still give an indication on their dustier shelves of how many editions of Wordsworth competed in the thirty years after his death. Some were illustrated and rather grandly printed; others went for cheapness and tiny double-columned print. But none of them included *The Prelude* for the simple reason that it was still protected by copyright.

The more important factor, however, was that there was a shift of emphasis in the perception of what the core of Wordsworth's achievement really was. Matthew Arnold's was the decisive voice. Arnold the poet, like the other writers just mentioned, had played his part in mediating Wordsworth to a later generation. The impact of Arnold the critic, however, was greater. In 1879 he made a selection of the poems, which he prefaced with a polemical essay on the nature of Wordsworth's greatness. Arnold's own poetic gravity and melancholy had taken much of its tone from Wordsworth. He had, literally, known the poet and after his death had written about him in many places, always assessing him in the company of only the greatest European writers. Arnold was a committed, though discriminating and not uncritical Wordsworthian. He carried authority. In the preface he argues that Wordsworth is not a philosopher, nor a religious teacher, and that those who have appropriated him as a moral guide have not only misjudged the poet but have created an idolatrous image of Wordsworth the Sage, diverting attention from the truth, which is that 'Wordsworth's poetry is great because of the extraordinary power with which Wordsworth feels the joy offered to us in nature, the joy offered to us in the simple primary affections and duties; and because of the extraordinary power with which, in case after case, he shows us this joy and renders it so as to make us share it'. This joy cannot be shared, Arnold declares, until we recognise that Wordsworth's 'formal philosophy' is an 'illusion'. It follows that neither *The Excursion* nor *The Prelude* is represented in Arnold's selection: 'His best work is in his shorter pieces.'

Arnold was well-intentioned. His aim was to effect a just evaluation, which would ensure Wordsworth's survival. But the effect of his essay and selection was malign. At a moment when critical theorists were conceding that poetry and philosophy were separate discourses and that the long poem was evidently a contradiction in terms, Arnold sanctioned partial, lazy reading and neglect of Wordsworth's most ambitious works. *The Excursion* still languishes unread on library shelves; *The Prelude* did not take its central place in the canon until the next century.

The disclosure of *The Prelude*

When *The Prelude* was approached it was at first through biography. F. W. H. Myers's *Wordsworth* (1880) for John Morley's very successful 'English Men of Letters' series was, as he admitted, little more than a rehash of Christopher Wordsworth's *Memoirs*, and although William Knight's massive *Life of William Wordsworth* (1889) looks more scholarly, it is in fact little more than a documented expansion of the life limned by the *Memoirs*. In both of these biographies *The Prelude* is quarried for apt descriptive quotation and nothing more. Their superficiality became apparent with the publication of Emile Legouis' *La Jeunesse de William Wordsworth* (Paris, 1896), translated by J. W.

Matthews as *The Early Life of William Wordsworth* (1897).
Sub-titled, 'A Study of *The Prelude*', Legouis' book ex-
amines Wordsworth's life and work from birth to 1798,
paralleling in its structure the narrative trajectory of *The
Prelude* itself. It is a pioneering work of scholarship, the first
to establish just how crucial were Wordsworth's experiences
in France. But though Legouis contextualises and footnotes
The Prelude, he does not treat it as a poem, that is as an
imaginative creation, and neither did George McLean Harper
in his *William Wordsworth; His Life, Works, and Influence*
(1916), the most wide-ranging and intelligent study which had
yet appeared.

Given that both Legouis and Harper presented *The Prelude*
essentially as a source of biographical information, ques-
tionable in detail but trustworthy in its overall presentation of
the growth of the poet's mind, it is striking that it should have
been they who discovered the poem's major lacuna and thus
opened up the whole question of Wordsworth's handling of
the materials of his own life. In the Harper biography, and
then in his *Wordsworth's French Daughter* (Princeton, 1921)
and Legouis' *William Wordsworth and Annette Vallon*
(1922), details emerged of the most important fact about the
poet's sojourn in France, on which both *The Prelude* and
Christopher Wordsworth (who knew the truth) had been
silent, namely, that Wordsworth had fathered a child with
Annette Vallon.

Not suprisingly interest in Wordsworth picked up. The
revelation was timely confirmation of Lytton Strachey's
demonstration in *Eminent Victorians* (1918) that many a
revered nineteenth-century sage had feet of clay. What price
now Arnold's claim that Wordsworth's greatness rested on
his celebration of 'the simple primary affections and duties'?
But the interest generated was focussed on the man, on the
biography of the poet rather than on the poet's use of his
biography. *The Prelude* remained a poem through which one
looked for the 'real' Wordsworth, a process which entailed
fleshing out the deficiencies of the text with knowledge drawn
from other sources. For some critics, notably Herbert Read,

Wordsworth (1930), Hugh I'Anson Faussett, *The Lost Leader* (1933), and, a late example, F. W. Bateson, *Wordsworth: A Re-Interpretation* (1954), Wordsworth was primarily a psychoanalytic subject and *The Prelude* a document in the case-study.

As so often happens, the poem as poem was rescued from this reductive approach by scholarship. In 1926 Ernest de Selincourt published an edition of *The Prelude*, in which the thirteen-book text of 1805, edited from manuscript, was displayed opposite the fourteen-book text of 1850. It was the most important moment in the poem's history since the publication of the first edition in 1850. Giving an account of all the manuscripts he believed extant, and recording variant readings generously in the *apparatus criticus* and notes, de Selincourt demonstrated that the poem had occupied Wordsworth throughout his most creative period, that it remained a concern for most of the rest of his life, and that it was central to any understanding of the place of *The Recluse* in Wordsworth's *œuvre*. The opening words of his introduction are, '*The Prelude* is the essential living document for the interpretation of Wordsworth's life and poetry.' De Selincourt's extensive notes also served an important function. Through his explication and citation of other poems he suggested implicitly that *The Prelude* was the key text, that even if all the rest of Wordsworth's poetry were to be lost, the essential Wordsworth would remain here. Most important of all, de Selincourt treated *The Prelude* as a poem, not just as a biographical document.

In 1959 Helen Darbishire issued a revised edition of de Selincourt's great text, which added substantially to understanding of the poem's genesis, for what she printed for the first time was the manuscript (called MS JJ) in which Wordsworth had drafted his earliest work in Germany over the winter 1798–9. Details were also given of the next manuscript (MS RV), which records a more developed but still early phase of composition.

The next stage in the presentation of the poem came about through a small but crucial change in vision. Although

Darbishire was familiar with all of the early *Prelude* manuscripts, her understanding of them was determined by a conviction established long before that all composition recorded in them was work *towards* the thirteen-book form. In 1970 Jonathan Wordsworth made the bold claim that this was not so ('The Growth of a Poet's Mind', *Cornell Library Journal*, 11 (1970), pp. 3–24). He argued that the early *Prelude* manuscripts represent a finished poem in two books, which was subsequently dismembered and incorporated into different versions of the autobiographical poem, which did not arrive at its thirteen-book form until other structures had been tried and abandoned. His argument is now generally accepted. The *Two-Part Prelude* of 1799, a poem whose identity de Selincourt and Darbishire would have denied, now has a secure place in the Wordsworth canon.

By disclosing the existence of a major poem which pre-dated the 1850 *Prelude* and revealing the mass of manuscript evidence on which study of both poems' evolution must be based, de Selincourt and Darbishire inserted into English literary history a work comparable in stature to *The Faerie Queene* or *Paradise Lost*. Theirs was a very great achievement, not only of diligent labour but of resourceful and imaginative scholarship. This must be stressed. The history of *The Prelude*'s 'after-life', until 1959 at least, is the history of the disclosure of the poem's identity. And the heroic agents of the story are not critics, biographers, or commentators, but the two scholars Ernest de Selincourt and Helen Darbishire. They also introduced a way of thinking about *The Prelude*, however, which has bedevilled critical discussion ever since 1926 and which only in the 1990s looks to be dying.

It seemed clear to de Selincourt that a reader faced with two long versions of *The Prelude* would want to decide which was the better of the two. Judging on some criteria, there could be, he declared, no argument: 'No one would doubt that the 1850 version is a better composition than the A [1805] text. Weak phrases are strengthened, and its whole texture is more closely knit' (p. xliv). Repeatedly, however, de Selincourt reverses this judgement, suggesting that such stylistic criteria are not the most important ones, and that not even in point of style is the 1850 *Prelude* always superior. And on higher grounds the 1805 version is to be preferred. In it the 'true disciple' will 'recognize the unmistakeable ring of sincerity in style'. He or she will also recognize truth to original inspiration, early philosophical positions untouched by later orthodoxy, political utterances not muted by conservative second thoughts. Even in his discussion of 'The ideal text of *The Prelude*' (pp. 1–li) de Selincourt leans towards 1805. An 'ideal text' would be constructed from the manuscripts presented in 1926 for the first time, 'but it would reject those later excrescences of a manner less pure, at times even meretricious, which are out of key with the spirit in which the poem was first conceived and executed. Most firmly would it reject all modifications of his original thought and theme.'

The battle, whose lines are drawn out here, was joined. Many American scholars and critics preferred the later text. One of the most important books yet written on Wordsworth, Geoffrey Hartman's *Wordsworth's Poetry 1787–1814* (1964), notably used the last revised text of the whole canon, despite the gesture towards history and chronological specificity in its title. British critics have tended to follow de Selincourt's lead, none more outspokenly than Jonathan Wordsworth who misses no occasion in his *William Wordsworth: The Borders of Vision* (1982) to point out the weakness of the 1850 text. In the revisions to the 'Climbing of Snowdon', for example, it is claimed, 'Wordsworth does not merely destroy one of his greatest pieces of poetry, he weakens precisely those aspects which had made it the fitting climax to his poem'. The poet of the 1850 *Prelude*, Jonathan Wordsworth declares, is 'in full retreat' (p. 328). In 1970 'The Norton *Prelude*' included a section entitled '1850 versus 1805', which concludes by quoting de Selincourt's judgement in favour of the 1805 version. As late as 1984 a whole session of the Wordsworth Conference at Grasmere was given over to a debate on the relative merits of 1805 and 1850, each 'team' passionately arguing for victory.

The debate has not been completely sterile, for it has at

least encouraged devotees of each poem to study carefully the merits of the other, but it is clearly stalled, because its terms still rest on de Selincourt's notion that 1805 and 1850 are the only two states of *The Prelude* with which criticism need seriously be concerned. Ever since its first volume appeared in 1975, however, the *Cornell Wordsworth* series has been demonstrating that statements about the 'best' or 'ideal' text of any Wordsworth poem can never be securely grounded. The volumes devoted to *The Prelude* reveal this truth most clearly of all. The poem was not conceived in an 1805 form; it did not rest in it when the thirteen-book structure did evolve; the 1850 text is not a version of 1805, but the latest stage in a series of fresh compositions. There are, in short, lots of *Prelude*s. The sheer weight of evidence, Jack Stillinger has recently argued, dictates that critics must 'grant the legitimacy and interest, intrinsic or in connection with other texts, of *all* the versions of *The Prelude* and the rest of the poems in the canon' ('Textual Primitivism and the Editing of Wordsworth', *Studies in Romanticism*, 28 (1989), pp. 3–28).

The implications of this declaration are dizzying. Students cannot possibly read all of the versions of *The Prelude* assembled by the Cornell editors. There will always be a need for one text for student use and this book has worked on the conviction that it ought to be the 1805 poem. But Stillinger is clearly right and his article is a promising sign that advanced study of *The Prelude* is entering a new phase. Future criticism, based on examination of all states of the text, will be able to substantiate more fully than ever before the truth of de Selincourt's observation that '*The Prelude* is the essential living document for the interpretation of Wordsworth's life and poetry'.

Conclusion

This book opened with the assertion that *The Prelude* is a Landmark of World Literature. It must close, however, with some consideration of the fact that this landmark has had little or no influence on later literature.

Wordsworth, of course, demonstrably has. Though each of them eventually disavowed this father figure, Keats, Shelley, and Byron were all profoundly influenced both by Wordsworth's poetry and by the image of the heroic poet he projected in his early life. The degree of Hopkins's indebtedness is most succinctly conveyed by his remark that he believed on the day the *Intimations Ode* was written, 'St George and St Thomas of Canterbury wore roses in heaven for England's sake' (letter to R. W. Dixon, 23 October 1886). Through Arnold and Ruskin and George Eliot and Pater, Wordsworthian attitudes and values were mediated in different genres to later generations. In the present state of knowledge it is not possible to make confident statements about T. S. Eliot's indebtedness to Wordsworth, but it is hard to believe that he was unconscious of his great precursor when he mused in this passage on 'spots of time':

Why, for all of us, out of all that we have heard, seen, felt, in a lifetime, do certain images recur, charged with emotion, rather than others? The song of one bird, the leap of one fish, at a particular place and time, the scent of one flower, an old woman on a German mountain path, six ruffians seen through an open window playing cards at night at a small French railway junction where there was a water-mill: such memories may have symbolic value, but of what we cannot tell, for they come to represent the depths of feeling into which we cannot peer.

('Conclusion' to *The Use of Poetry and The Use of Criticism*)

One might affirm Wordsworth's stature in world literature, also, simply by considering his stature within the Romantic Movement. Grand phrases ought to be anathema to all academic writers and readers, but it is difficult to avoid a certain grandiloquence when one considers Romanticism. Across European and American cultures, manifesting itself in diverse ways in politics, economics, law, as well as in the arts, Romanticism shaped the modern world and its effects are still being registered today. Introducing his comprehensive study, *The Creative Imagination*, James Engell declares, 'There is really nothing with which to compare it. . . The idea of imagination, developed in the Enlightenment and triumphant in Romanticism, marks the end of an epoch stretching back 2500 years and introduces a new stage of thought and letters, now two hundred years in progress' (pp. 4, 6). Wordsworth is one of the dominant factors in the British and American dimension to Romanticism's triumph.

Moving from history to the present day, it is worth registering that Wordsworth is now enshrined as one of the two greatest poets of the English tradition, Shakespeare, of course, being the other. This fact might be established by a laborious parade of statistics – the number of Wordsworth texts sold, a survey of university syllabuses, the number of visitors to Dove Cottage in Grasmere annually, and so on. But it can also be made through what might look at first like a trivial anecdote. In the late 1980s British television ran an advertisement for Heineken lager, which featured a poet, striding across hills, struggling to get a line of poetry right. Once refreshed by a draught of Heineken, he hit on it easily – the first line of 'Daffodils', 'I wandered lonely as a cloud'. Consider the significance of this. The creators of the advertisement judged that they could rely on instant recognition both of poet and poem by a mass audience, most of whom would not have read a line of Wordsworth. Wordsworth can be joked about – witness the BBC's very successful comedy series *The Wordsmiths of Gorsemere* – and 'Daffodils' is a favourite with cartoonists, but what is acknowledged in the joking is that the poet has become a national monument. Poking fun at Wordsworth is like joking about Queen Victoria. It concedes the massive presence of a shaping force in national culture.

The point needs no reinforcement. Wordsworth is one of the greatest writers of the Romantic period, one of our greatest poets, and *The Prelude* is his masterpiece. It is quite discomfiting, therefore, that nothing further or more specific can be asserted about *The Prelude* itself and later literature. Primarily because of the belatedness of its publication and eventual recognition, the poem has not had the influence it would have had, were its publication date 1805 rather than 1850.

It is tempting to think that the so-called 'confessional' poetry of the later twentieth century – Lowell, Berryman, Plath, Sexton and others – must owe something to *The Prelude*. From *Life Studies* through to *Notebook* and *History* Robert Lowell, for example, engages in a poetic project remarkably like Wordsworth's. Exploring passages of his own life, and in the later volumes disclosing detail with astonishing lack of reserve, Lowell reshapes volumes just as Wordsworth did, as if the poems are so integral to the lived life that they have to change as it does. Just as Wordsworth deploys Dorothy Wordsworth, Coleridge, Mary Hutchinson, Raisley Calvert, and others in *The Prelude*, so Lowell deploys (some would say exploits) his former wife and children, transgressing continually and bewilderingly the boundary between life and art. Somewhere far distant behind this poetry Wordsworth undoubtedly stands, but dominating the foreground is Walt Whitman and *Leaves of Grass*, another poet who remoulded his greatest work to make it commensurate with the grandeur of his own self-projection.

It is equally tempting to trace back the line of twentieth-century poetry which celebrates the ordinary, which recognizes the poet's duty, as T. S. Eliot put it, 'to make poetry out of the unexplored resources of the unpoetical' ('What Dante Means to Me' in *To Criticize the Critic*). Eliot's remark recalls Wordsworth's earliest radical pronouncement on poetry, the 'Advertisement' to the first edition of *Lyrical Ballads* in 1798, in which he pugnaciously insisted that the definition of 'poetical' must be enlarged to include simple language and commonplace subject matter. But though the work of, for example, Hardy, Edward Thomas, Robert Frost, and Seamus Heaney continues in form, diction, and subject matter, a line that stretches back to Wordsworth, the seminal poetry is the lyrics of *Lyrical Ballads* and *Poems, in Two Volumes*, not *The Prelude*.

No introduction to a great poem should end on such a *diminuendo* note and two further observations might properly be made. The first is that it is possible for a work of literature to be both so original and so complete in its artistic realization that it remains for a long time an object of admiration, without being a creative model. *Finnegans Wake* and *Tristram Shandy* would be examples; *The Wreck of the 'Deutschland'* another. It may be *The Prelude* is such a poem. The second observation follows from this. It is that 'influence' in literary history is not predictable. It obeys no rules of probability and is heedless of time. The strongest influence on some of the finest poetry of the twentieth century, T. S. Eliot's, is Dante. It may be that *The Prelude* will present itself to some future poet as a resource of creative possibilities after a similar lapse of time.

Guide to further reading

This reading list does not include articles nor general books on Wordsworth, except those which have particularly useful sections on *The Prelude*. For full bibliographies of all published writings on Wordsworth see below. Place of publication is London unless otherwise noted.

1. Bibliography

Comprehensive lists of all Wordsworth scholarship are now available. The student should begin with Mark Jones and Karl Kroeber, *Wordsworth Scholarship and Criticism 1973–1984: An Annotated Bibliography* (New York, 1985), which gives reference back to preceding bibliographies.

2. Editions

The standard edition of the poems remains *The Poetical Works of William Wordsworth*, ed. Ernest de Selincourt and Helen Darbishire (5 vols. Oxford, 1940–9). The accompanying volume *The Prelude*, ed. Ernest de Selincourt (1926), 2nd revised edn ed. Helen Darbishire (Oxford, 1959) is still of use. The de Selincourt-Darbishire edition is being superseded, however, by the multi-volume *Cornell Wordsworth*, general editor Stephen Parrish (Ithaca, 1975 –). Fourteen volumes have appeared at the time of writing and they are indispensable for serious study. Volumes devoted to *The Prelude* are, *The Prelude, 1798–1799*, ed. Stephen Parrish (Ithaca, 1977), *The Fourteen-Book Prelude*, ed. W. J. B. Owen (Ithaca, 1985), *The Thirteen-Book Prelude*, ed. Mark L. Reed (Ithaca, 1991). For student use the following editions can be recommended. *The Prelude 1799, 1805, 1850*, ed. Jonathan Wordsworth, M. H. Abrams, and Stephen Gill (New York, 1979), often referred to as the 'Norton *Prelude*'. *William Wordsworth*, ed. Stephen Gill (1984), a generous selection of poetry and prose in the *Oxford Authors* series. Other standard editions are: *The Prose Works of William Wordsworth*, ed. W. J. B. Owen and Jane Worthington Smyser (3 vols., Oxford, 1974); *Letters of William and Dorothy Wordsworth*, ed. E. de

Selincourt; *The Early Years, 1787–1805*, revised Chester L. Shaver (Oxford, 1967); *The Middle Years, 1806–1811*, revised Mary Moorman (Oxford, 1969); *The Middle Years, 1812–1820*, revised Mary Moorman and Alan G. Hill (Oxford, 1970); *The Later Years, 1821–1853*, revised Alan G. Hill (4 vols. Oxford, 1978–88).

3. Biography

Christopher Wordsworth, *Memoirs of William Wordsworth* (2 vols., 1851). F. W. H. Myers, *Wordsworth (1880)*. William Knight, *Life of William Wordsworth* (3 vols., 1889). Emile Legouis, *La Jeunesse de William Wordsworth* (Paris, 1896), trans. J. W. Matthews, *The Early Life of William Wordsworth* (1897). Emile Legouis, *William Wordsworth and Annette Vallon* (1922). George McLean Harper, *William Wordsworth; His Life, Works, and Influence* (2 vols., 1916). George McLean Harper, *Wordsworth's French Daughter* (Princeton, 1921). Stephen Gill, *William Wordsworth: A Life* (Oxford, 1989). Ben Ross Schneider, Jr, *Wordsworth's Cambridge Education* (Cambridge, 1957). Robert Gittings and Jo Manton, *Dorothy Wordsworth* (Oxford, 1985). Richard Holmes, *Coleridge: Early Visions* (1989), the first of two volumes. Donald E. Hayden, *Wordsworth's Walking Tour of 1790* (Tulsa, Okla., 1983); *Wordsworth's Travels in Wales and Ireland* (Tulsa, Okla., 1985), both invaluable topographical-biographical aids to reading *The Prelude*.

Context: political, social, aesthetic

The following in various ways will help the student situate *The Prelude* in its historical context. *Henry Crabb Robinson On Books and Their Writers*, ed. Edith J, Morley (3 vols., 1938). Basil Willey, *The Eighteenth-Century Background* (1940). S. T. Coleridge, *Lectures 1795 on Politics and Religion*, ed. Lewis Patton and Peter Mann (1971). James Engell, *The Creative Imagination: Enlightenment to Romanticism* (Cambridge, Mass., 1981). Albert Goodwin, *The Friends of Liberty: The English Democratic Movement in the Age of the French Revolution* (1979). Nicholas Roe, *Wordsworth and Coleridge: The Radical Years* (Oxford, 1988). Marilyn Butler, *Burke, Paine, Godwin, and the Revolution Controversy* (Cambridge, 1984). Jonathan Wordsworth, Michael C. Jaye, and Robert Woof, *William Wordsworth and the Age of English Romanticism* (New Brunswick and London, 1987). H. W. Piper, *The Active Universe: Pantheism and the Concept of Imagination in the English Romantic Poets* (1962). Carl Woodring, *Politics in English Romantic Poetry* (Cambridge, Mass., 1970). Max Byrd, *London*

Transformed: Images of the City in the Eighteenth Century (New Haven, 1978). Richard Altick, *The Shows of London* (Cambridge, Mass., 1978). Ronald Paulson, *Representations of Revolution, 1789–1820* (New Haven, 1983).

Language

Francis Austin, *The Language of Wordsworth and Coleridge* (1989). Hugh Sykes Davies, *Wordsworth and the Worth of Words*, ed. John Kerrigan and Jonathan Wordsworth (Cambridge, 1987). Olivia Smith, *The Politics of Language 1791–1819* (Oxford, 1984). Josephine Miles, *Wordsworth and the Vocabulary of Emotion* (Berkeley, 1942). Donald Davie, *Articulate Energy: An Inquiry into the Syntax of English Poetry* (1955). Christopher Ricks, *The Force of Poetry* (Oxford, 1984). Christopher Ricks, 'Wordsworth: "A Pure Organic Pleasure from the Lines" ', *Essays in Criticism*, 21 (1971), pp. 1–32. Thomas De Quincey, 'Jeffrey, Wordsworth, and Coleridge', in *De Quincey as Critic*, ed. John E. Jordan (1973).

Scholarship and criticism

M. H. Abrams, *Natural Supernaturalism: Tradition and Revolution in Romantic Literature* (New York, 1971). Herbert Lindenberger, *On Wordsworth's 'Prelude'* (Princeton, 1963). Herbert Lindenberger, 'The Reception of *The Prelude*', *Bulletin of the New York Public Library*, 64 (1960), pp. 196–208. Lee Erickson, 'The Egoism of Authorship: Wordsworth's Poetic Career', *Journal of English and Germanic Philology*, 89 (1990), pp. 37–50. Jack Stillinger, 'Textual Primitivism and the Editing of Wordsworth', *Studies in Romanticism*, 28 (1989), pp. 3–28. Richard J. Onorato, *The Character of the Poet: Wordsworth in 'The Prelude'* (Princeton, 1971). Thomas McFarland, *Romanticism and the Forms of Ruin: Wordsworth, Coleridge, and the Modalities of Fragmentation* (Princeton, 1981). Geoffrey H. Hartman, *Wordsworth's Poetry 1787–1814* (New Haven, 1970). Robert Rehder, *Wordsworth and the Beginnings of Modern Poetry* (1981). David Ellis, *Wordsworth, Freud and the Spots of Time: Interpretation in 'The Prelude'* (Cambridge, 1985). Jonathan Wordsworth, *William Wordsworth: The Borders of Vision* (Oxford, 1982). Jonathan Wordsworth, *The Music of Humanity* (1969). *'The Prelude': A Selection of Critical Essays*, ed. W. J. Harvey and Richard Gravil (1972). Mary Jacobus, *Romanticism Writing and Sexual Difference: Essays on 'The Prelude'* (Oxford, 1989). James K. Chandler, *Wordsworth's Second Nature: A Study of the Poetry and Politics* (Chicago, 1984). Kenneth R. Johnston, *Wordsworth and 'The Recluse'* (New Haven, 1984). Alan Liu, *Wordsworth: The Sense of History* (Stanford, 1989).